DISCOVERING A LIFE WITHOUT LIMITS:
How cancer took my sight,
blindness gave me vision,
and the mountains let me live.

walnutstreetpublishing.com

Copyright © 2021 Kyle Coon

All rights reserved.

DISCOVERING A LIFE WITHOUT LIMITS:
How cancer took my sight, blindness gave me vision, and the mountains let me live.

KYLE COON

Table of Contents

Acknowledgements	i
Foreword	v
Letter to the Reader	ix
Eye Cancer	1
Yes I Can, Sir	11
School Daze	20
Rock Jock	31
Global Explorers	41
Cusco, Peru	46
The Inca Trail	56
Ending and Beginning	64
The Right Moves	81
Big Mountain	96
The Climb	105
Summit Fever	115
True Companion	124
The Beginning of Team Sight Unseen	140
Success! Without a Summit?	148
Love is Blind	165
Welcome TO THE Real World	176
Epilogue: Time to Tri	188

Acknowledgements

I have been truly privileged to be surrounded by a wealth of talented and inspirational friends, family, and mentors from the time I was born. While it would be impossible to list and thank all of those who have impacted my life, I promise that you're in my heart and thoughts. Rest assured, I am where I am today because of the faith, love, and caring of so many special individuals.

First and foremost, thank you to my family for raising me to uphold the values that have made me into the person I am today.

I am indebted to the wonderful doctors and nurses at Will's Eye Hospital, Nemours Children's Hospital, and Wolfson Children's Hospital. I would not be here if it were not for your passion and dedication to helping me fight and triumph over cancer and allowing me a chance at life.

Thank you to the entire Norville family: Lee, Susan, Charlie, Claire, and John. You guys are my second family.

Thank you to Candy Clark and her deceased husband, "Devildog" Dan. Apart from teaching me how to enjoy being dragged behind a motorboat on an inner tube—at extremely high speeds—you connected my family to the Weihenmayer's.

To Ed Weihenmayer, who introduced me to Erik and who has been a steadfast supporter and mentor. Thank you to Erik Weihenmayer for entering my life and providing me with just a few words of inspiration to put me on the path to living my life without limits. Thanks also for just being a great friend.

To Eric Alexander and Jeff Evans. You guys helped me realize the importance of solid teamwork and always stepping up to be a leader.

Thank you to the Karst family: "Coach," Tom, Jen, Thomas, Matt, and Pete. You taught me the finer points of rock climbing and infected me with a love of climbing.

To the Henderson family: David, Karan, and Katelyn. It's hard to forget all the good times at climbing competitions and on great outdoor climbing trips to Georgia, Tennessee, and North Carolina.

Thank you to No Barriers for putting on the Leading The Way Program. To tell the truth, you inspired this book.

Thank you to Team Sight Unseen: Justin Grant, Brad Jaffke, Peter Green, Joseph Mayfield, and Ben Meyer. You are my rope team, friends, and brothers in the mountains. We really should not allow such lengthy periods between climbs. Let's continue to show the world that "It's not the destination but the journey that makes the trip worthwhile."

Thank you to Robert Levitt for teaching me how to downhill ski so I could experience the mountains in a whole new way.

Thank you to Dave and Barbara Gadbaw for being my ski guides for so long. But, more importantly, thank you for being such amazing family friends. I can't wait to go "tree skiing" again.

Thank you to Ken Chertow for refining my wrestling technique and showing me that "athletes compete with each other and champions compete with themselves."

To the numerous schoolteachers:

- Susan Duzenberry for teaching me braille.
- Barbara Irving (first and second-grade), Teresa Drane (elementary orientation and mobility), and Betsy Dando (third through fifth grade) for challenging me to succeed in my early education.
- Susan Kahn (eighth through tenth-grade vision teacher) for going above and beyond the call of duty to make sure I was successful.
- Karlin Michelson (sixth through twelfth-grade orientation and mobility instructor)—for helping give and refine my skills as a cane and guide-dog traveler so I could be independent.
- Numerous teachers at James Weldon Johnson College Preparatory Middle School, you made me realize how fun education could be with a little creativity.
- The teachers of Paxon School for Advanced Studies: Despite all the sleepless nights, long essays, and Advanced Placement

Exams, you opened up worlds of opportunity that I never thought possible.

To the University of Central Florida for accepting me, bending over backward to accommodate me, and helping me to launch into the world. The lessons I learned were not all academic. Charge on Knights!

Thanks to Joan McCain, not just for helping me to write this book, but for being a great friend and adviser. Thanks for assembling a great team of students to help me share my story with the world. That was easily my favorite college class.

Thanks, "Team Kyle." Samantha Dilday, Sophia Farkis, Nicholas Osler, Francesca Parker, Nick Rourke, Devin Shoemaker, Adam Sheikh, Heather Waymouth, and Leann Yutuc. Your hard work, enthusiasm, and dedication to this project are finally recognized. Thank you very much to the United States Military servicemen and women. You make it possible for me and many others to live free and blessed lives in the greatest country on Earth.

A special thanks to the United States Marine Corps. Through the teachings of the USMC, my father was able to raise his children to uphold the values of honor, courage, and integrity. It was also through the connection of the Marine Corps that I first met Ed and Erik Weihenmayer, as well as so many other great friends who have helped me when I've been in a bind.

Semper Fidelis and OOH RAH!

And, last but most certainly not least, thanks to YOU for taking time out of your busy life to pick up and read this book. I'm fortunate in that I have a story to tell. And, if I'm lucky, maybe my words will touch a few of you and inspire you to embrace your adversity and live your life without limits.

Foreword

I've known Kyle since he was seven years old, not long after he received his cancer diagnosis and the removal of his eyes. Kyle's dad reached out to my dad since both are Marines, and he could, of course, empathize with their situation. We arranged to meet in Jacksonville, FL, when I was giving a presentation in the area.

At first, Kyle was a little boy who was shy and introverted, which is perfectly understandable given all that he had been through. In just a few months, he had gone from being able to see to total blindness. I could also empathize because I was a new parent at the time and could imagine what it would be like for my daughter to face such adversity.

When you're a kid, blindness is like a brick wall that you don't know how to get through. On the other side is total darkness and uncertainty. You don't know what you can do; you're unprepared—it's like you have been hit on the head with a baseball bat, and you are just stunned. So, it made sense to me that Kyle had withdrawn into himself.

After hearing my talk about climbing Everest, Kyle started to open up and ask lots of questions. He became very inquisitive about blindness and how to deal with it, excitedly asking me how I did different activities like climbing, skiing, and skydiving. That seemed to be just the inspiration he needed to get started adapting to a world without eyesight.

As I followed his progress over the years, I was impressed by how Kyle adjusted to blindness and began pushing the envelope. This son of a Marine really came out of his shell and bulldogged his way through lots of barriers. Not only did Kyle excel in school, but he also became class president, joined the climbing club and wrestling team, learned to ski, and got his first guide dog.

Several years after our first meeting, I appeared on The Oprah Show as a guest to discuss the theme of "impacts you have made that you don't know." What I didn't know was Oprah had arranged for Kyle to make a surprise appearance!

Kyle read an emotional letter that he had written to me in Braille about my influence on his life. There I was on national television crying —much to the delight of Oprah and her audience!

When I helped start a new program called Leading The Way, run by an organization called No Barriers, Kyle was on our first program to Machu Picchu via the Super Inca Trail in the Peruvian Andes. Our group of blind and sighted students took the road less traveled and, in the process, became a super strong team. Along the way, we painted a schoolhouse in a remote village; we were a great team as we worked hard not to paint over the blackboard and windows. As we crested the ridge into Machu Picchu, we felt we had forged a desire among the students to make a real impact in the world.

Since that trip, Kyle teamed up with some of those blind students to climb mountains around the world, including Kilimanjaro, the highest peak in Africa. Calling themselves "Team Sight Unseen," their mission is to inspire both blind/visually impaired people and those with normal sight.

Kyle truly represents the No Barriers mindset. Even though we all face challenges in life—whether you are blind or not—he demonstrates that we can tackle them head-on with the right tools and a good team. Kyle proves that despite adversity, we all can live a life with purpose. He is the embodiment of the No Barriers motto, "What's inside of us is stronger than what's in our way."

I am a huge fan and supporter of Kyle and believe you will be too once you read his story. There is no question that he will succeed at anything he sets his mind to because of his right attitude and grit. He's only in his twenties now, so the sequel to this book in a few decades should be even more spectacular!

— Erik Weihenmayer

Letter to the Reader

Dear Reader,

Reading books has been part of my life since I was a little kid. Whether it was my parents, sisters, or teachers reading me a book; listening to a book on tape, CD, or digitally; or, using my fingertips to read a book in Braille, I've found the written and spoken word to be powerful.

It must have been 2007 or so when teachers, family, and friends started telling me I should write a book. Or they'd say they couldn't wait until I wrote a book. I humored everyone and said I would write a book. Maybe I could be an author and inspire and motivate generations of people with my words. I dreamed of grandeur, book tours, book signings, being on talk shows. In short, I dreamt of writing a book for what I now see as the wrong reasons.

As the years passed, I wrote down my experiences. I formed them into something resembling a book and then let it sit on my computer for years. It never seemed the right time to publish. Of course, now I realize that's because the reasons why I was writing the book weren't the best. I was obsessed with perfection. I was unsatisfied with the ending. What if another major event happened that I had to document? Shouldn't it be part of the book?

It took a long time to understand that just because a book ends doesn't mean the story is over. It also took me a long time to truly understand why I wanted, or why I should, share my story with the world in the form of a book.

What you are going to read is just the beginning of my story because I'm still writing chapters. Hopefully, I can put those chapters together and make an even better book than this.

I chose to call this book "Discovering a Life Without Limits" because everything I recount in these pages is just that. It's me discovering who I am as a person, a writer, an athlete. It's me discovering how to push the limits of what I and others think is possible. It's me discovering that I'm nothing special, and yet every person in this world is special. This book is just highlighting the beginning of my journey.

We all pick up and read a book for different reasons. I read to be entertained, to learn, to find inspiration or motivation. I don't know your reasons for picking up this book. My hope is that while you read through, you are entertained, you learn something, or you find just a smidgen of inspiration or motivation. More than that, though, when you finish reading this book, I hope you put it down and say, "What's next for me?" I hope you are curious to begin discovering your own life without limits.

Chapter 1

Eye Cancer

In 1492, Columbus sailed the ocean blue.

We hold these truths to be self-evident, that all men are created equal, that they are endowed by their creator with certain unalienable rights, that among these are life, liberty, and the pursuit of happiness.

Four score and seven years ago, our fathers brought forth on this continent a new nation, conceived in liberty and dedicated to the proposition that all men are created equal.

Your son has cancer.

    I was a history nut from a very early age. I loved learning about what people in the past did, how they did it, and why they did it. While the histories I read way back were fun and entertaining, I now know that your past forms you. Or rather, our past provides us with the tools, opportunity, and understanding to shape ourselves into the people we are and the people we want to be.

    Your son has cancer.

    They were shocked, scared, helpless. I can only imagine how my parents felt when the doctor sat them down at the University of Chicago Medical Center and spoke those words. There we were. Dad, barely two years removed from the Marine Corps and holding me. And Mom, holding my two-year-old sister Cassandra on her lap, and almost three months pregnant with my little sister, Kelsey. I was 10 months old—a baby. Babies did not get cancer. However, the doctor continued.

    "The only hope we have to save his life is to remove his eyes. I have scheduled him for surgery on Tuesday," he said on Friday.

Chance Encounters

Neither of my parents were strangers to challenges, hard work, or adversity.

Steven Coon was the oldest of four. He grew up working on his family's farm, then helping out on his best friend's farm when he got into high school. A natural athlete, my Dad played point guard on his high school basketball team. Not being the type of person who found enjoyment in the pursuit of academics, at age 17, he made a decision and enlisted in the US Marine Corps. In the summer of 1984, he shipped off to San Diego, California, for boot camp. It would be nearly four years before he met Ann Marie Paluch.

Ann Marie was an honors student, member of the dance and cheerleading squads, and good friends with Sheryl Coon—Steve's youngest sister. She was the youngest of three, her parents owned their own business, and Ann's father, Joseph Paluch, was the President of the International Association of Refrigerated Warehousing. Ann learned the meaning of hard work through her parents, competition with her siblings, and school. Being a dedicated student, Ann excelled in academics and graduated a semester early from high school, taking extra classes each morning before school. She planned to spend her last semester of high school studying abroad in France before attending Arizona State University in the fall.

Sheryl Coon invited Ann to a New Year's Eve party that her older brother, who was home on leave from the Marines, was throwing. "He's stationed in Arizona, and since you're going to go to ASU, you might as well start meeting people who are out there," Sheryl said. So, Ann—not being a major party animal—agreed to go to the party. Lucky for me and my Dad, that she did.

Sheryl introduced Ann to Steve, and the two got to talking. They sat at a table and talked for more than four hours. The only times they were not talking was when my Dad would go to replace his empty beer with a fresh one. This was very unusual, considering that Steve had always been the life and soul of the party, and now he was off to the side talking with one girl and enjoying it.

When Steve went back to Arizona, Ann wrote him a letter saying, "I hope you don't just see me as your little sister's friend." And that was it. They started corresponding by writing letters to each other over six months. They spent almost all their time together when Steve came home on leave in June, and soon after, Ann moved out to Arizona to go to school. She spent the summer semester at Arizona State but then transferred to Arizona Western College in Yuma, Arizona, where Steve was stationed. On August 2, 1988, Ann Marie's eighteenth birthday, Steve asked her to marry him. And on August 17— fifteen days later — they were married. Their families would find out in October when Ann's parents came out for a visit.

A year after eloping, Steve and Ann Marie had a daughter, Cassandra. The following year Steve received his honorable discharge from the Marines after having served six years and deciding it was time to take his family and life in a new direction. They moved back to Chicago, Illinois, and a year after, I came along. My younger sister, Kelsey, followed a year and a half after me and eight years after her, our baby sister Caitlin. In October 1992, my parents faced the biggest challenge, hardship, and adversity of their young lives.

Unfair Treatment

I had bilateral sporadic retinoblastoma. Retinoblastoma is a rare eye cancer found in young children as early as a few months to as late as three to four years. My particular diagnosis meant that I had the disease in both eyes, and since I had no family history, it was a "sporadic" genetic mutation. I received my diagnosis late, and the cancer was progressing quickly. My parents decided to sleep on it and see what they could find out for themselves. They called to tell the family the news of my cancer diagnosis, and later that night, a family friend called my parents and told them of a doctor in Philadelphia, Pennsylvania. This doctor was known for his work with retinoblastoma. My parents contacted Will's Eye Hospital in Philadelphia and scheduled a consultation on Monday. My parents often tell me—and others—that they do not remember that weekend particularly well. The day after my diagnosis, they stood up at their close friends' wedding, and then on Monday, they were on a plane with me flying from Chicago to Philly.

My parents met with Doctors Jerry and Carol Shields, a husband-and-wife duo world renown for their work with retinoblastoma. The Child Social Worker that worked for Will's Eye sat my parents down and explained to them. "Look, we see all the toughest cases here. The Shields make it their top priority to save lives and preserve as much sight as possible."

For some reason, my Dad seemed satisfied. He sat back, looked at Mom, and said, "We're in the right place."

"How can you tell?" Mom asked.

Without hesitation, Dad replied, "Carol Shields went to Notre Dame; she's got to be good."

After my initial examination with the Shields, they informed my parents that they felt very confident that they could preserve a great deal of my vision despite the progression of the disease. My parents decided to do my treatment in Philadelphia. Returning to Chicago, they packed us up for an extended stay in Philly. We moved into the Ronald McDonald House in October, and I underwent treatment immediately. We lived at the Ronald McDonald House for three months while I was going in for treatment. I was going through intense radiation and chemotherapy treatment. The good news was that I was responding, or seemed to be.

We moved back to Chicago just in time for Christmas, and then my Dad started talking with a man in the warehousing business. Dad had been working for Mom's dad, and Grandpa Joe had taught Dad a lot about the warehousing industry. My Dad had started to excel and caught the attention of Billy Morris, who was looking to open a cold storage warehouse in Jacksonville, Florida. He offered my Dad a position helping him manage the warehouses, and my Dad saw a tremendous opportunity for growth. He accepted the offer, and we began looking for a home, schools, and a hospital that would work with my doctors in Philadelphia to continue treatment.

We found them all and moved to Jacksonville, Florida, in July of 1993. We were a family of five: Mom, Dad, Cassandra, myself, and

Kelsey—who was only a couple of months old. Our closest family was in Chicago, Dad had a new job, and I was regressing. The cancer was coming back.

Fortunately, though, we found dedicated doctors in Jacksonville at Wolfson Children's Hospital and Nemours Clinic who wanted to eradicate my cancer just as much as the Shields did up in Philly.

The fight continued.

Pills, Patches, Poles, and Ports

I don't have many memories from before the time I was three. Probably my earliest memories are going to preschool for the first time. I was already considered legally blind since cancer, radiation, and chemotherapy had taken a toll on my sight. My parents had to find a school that could accommodate any needs I may have. Also, the doctors had told my parents that I would go blind and encouraged them to make any necessary preparations to ensure that I could live the best and most independent life possible.

My parents enrolled me at Fishweir Elementary in Mrs. Susan's class. Fishweir Elementary was a regular elementary school with a "Vision Program." Kids from across the city of Jacksonville who were blind or visually impaired had the option of going to their neighborhood schools, Florida School for the Deaf and Blind (FSDB) located in St. Augustine, just a 45-minute drive away—or Fishweir. Many chose to attend either FSDB or Fishweir. Teachers who knew the needs of blind and visually impaired children could teach them Braille, enlarge documents, and teach them how to adapt to a sighted world.

Mrs. Susan was my preschool teacher, and she took it upon herself to not just teach me my print alphabet but my Braille one as well. It's funny to look back at preschool and think that I thought nothing of it. If anything, I thought Braille was fun to learn right along with print.

I went through two years of pre-kindergarten in Mrs. Susan's class. I was learning my letters and numbers in both Braille and print. I made friends, playing basketball with a little red plastic hoop and orange rubber balls by the classroom's front door. My two best friends were Cameron Range and Carlos Murray. We always argued over who was the best ballplayer—of course, it was me—and we always fought over who's turn it was to be Michael Jordan. Playing basketball with Cameron and Carlos, learning to read and write in print and Braille, I never thought I was different or special. I didn't know what blindness or cancer was. I was just Kyle.

It was not until my second year of pre-kindergarten and then again in kindergarten that I remember all the traveling. Every six to eight weeks, my Dad and I would board a plane or train and head up to Philadelphia. I would spend the weekend in treatment, and then on Monday or Tuesday, we would come home. Then in-between trips to Philadelphia, I would have appointments at Nemours or Wolfson's. I can't tell you how many drugs I was on or what procedures I had done on me at any given time, but I do know that it was a lot.

I remember taking oral chemotherapy almost nightly. I hated swallowing the little white pills. My parents would hide the pill in a tablespoon of orange or rainbow sherbet and then give it to me. I remember laying on the table in the doctor's office as drops were put into my eyes to dilate them so the doctors could look into them and see what was going on.

In Philadelphia, Dr. Shields would tape or sew radioactive material directly onto my eyeball. I was forced to lie on one side to allow gravity to pull the tumors over to that side and the radioactive "plaque" could do its work. However, try keeping a three, four, five-year-old kid still for very long. I would be allowed to go down to the playroom at the Ronald McDonald House and play for a short time each day if I behaved myself and didn't move, scream or cry.

Pills, drops, or eye patches, none of them were as bad as the needles. There were always needles, shots, IV poles, and bags. When I was younger, and it was time for me to "go to sleep" so the doctors could look at me and make me better, I would fight it. I kicked and screamed at the top of my lungs, "Please Mommy, please Daddy, don't let them take me! I hate the mask!" The "mask" was a rubber mask that fit over my nose and mouth and pumped some sort of anesthetic gas into my lungs, causing me to fall asleep.

Eventually, I graduated from the mask to the "Port." The "Port" was a catheter inserted into the left side of my chest just under my skin and not super noticeable, but I could feel it. It was a lump and not natural.

Before I went in for surgery or when I needed to get hooked up to an IV, the doctors and nurses would jab a needle into my port. My regular oncology nurse, Joney, called me "target practice" since I squirmed, flailed, and kicked so much that she had to get good at finding an opening and then sticking me perfectly with the needle. Sometimes Dad would even be the one to stick me at the hospital. It was a lot easier than me kicking and screaming.

For a while, the IV pole and drip bag seemed to be an extension of my body. I remember lying in the hospital bed watching movies on a tiny T.V. I remember grabbing for the pink "hurl bucket," as my Dad called it. The burning sensation of the chemo rushing up from my stomach into my throat and mouth was probably the worst. The throwing up, the smell, the crackle of the hospital bed sheets with each movement are all the sensations that make my skin crawl. At my worst, I would walk into the clinic, and the smell would hit me, and suddenly I would be doubled over, throwing up. However, at the same time, there were little moments of happiness where I didn't think about being sick.

In Philadelphia, I became friends with a young boy suffering from retinoblastoma as well. Antonio was from Italy, and neither he nor his parents spoke English. One day, my Mom was walking by the telephone in the Ronald McDonald house, and a man was talking very animatedly in another language. Mom approached and tried to ask the man if she could help. He began asking Mom questions in different languages until finally..." Parlez-vous français?"

Mom still remembered her high school French and learned that his son was very sick and needed to get to the hospital. Mom arranged for a cab to take Antonio and his parents to the hospital. Antonio and I would play together in the playroom at the Ronald McDonald house.

Toy cars, puppets, action figures, it didn't matter. For the time that we were together playing, neither of us was sick. I would later learn that Antonio didn't make it.

More than moments in the playroom, though, were the moments in my actual hospital room, the times when I was so far down in the dumps that all I wanted was just not to throw up. It was during that time when my Mom would read me stories. Together we would read "Mose the Fireman" or "Charlotte's Web." There were lots of books, lots of stories. And then there were the endless games of "Uno" and "Go Fish" with my Mom and sisters. Then Dad would arrive at the hospital, we would have dinner, and Mom would take Cassandra and Kelsey home, and Dad would spend the night on the couch in my hospital room. The following morning Dad would get up, and he and Mom would trade places while he went home or went to work.

Our only prayer was that I would get better. With every IV drip, with every blast of radiation, and with every heave of my stomach, the cancer was being purged from my body. And it was. But it came with a price.

In February 1997, my family decided to remove my left eye. The constant treatments of radiation and chemo had rendered my eye useless. I was five years old and going into kindergarten. Now all of a sudden, I had to be more careful. Only having one eye — after having two — was scary. Now I could only see half of what I had been able to see before. Coupled with being more injury-prone due to years of cancer treatment, I was not the most durable child. My kindergarten teacher, Mrs. Craig, kept a close eye on me, especially on the playground. However, in reality, I didn't slow down.

My best friend, John Norville, and I still had intense games of one-on-one basketball in the driveway of my house. I still ran, jumped, and tussled. I just had one eyeball. Yet, I was still going to the hospital, still doing treatment. I was still fighting.

Triple Rainbows

On October 9, 1998, I went in for my final surgery. My remaining eye was too damaged. And the cancer was relentless. The year leading up to my final surgery is memorable. The last month of my kindergarten year, my Dad took me to Chicago to see a Chicago Bulls game and to meet my favorite player, Michael Jordan. I sat on his lap, we snapped photos, and he gave me an autographed Bulls hat. I still have it in a Plexiglas case, and I carry the photo in my wallet.

In September of my first-grade year, a month before my last surgery, some family friends from our church had made it possible to send my family out to Montana to visit a dude ranch. It had been a long-time dream of mine to go to a dude ranch and ride horses. My parents wanted me to see the beauty of the Rocky Mountains and the beautiful changing colors of fall.

For one week in September, we went out for a week of horseback riding, fun, and adventure at Laughing Water Ranch. During that unforgettable week, there was one moment that sticks out in all our minds. We were driving back from a day spent at a ghost town in British Columbia, Canada. It had been a cloudy, rainy, and overcast day, but it cleared up on our way back to the ranch. Noticing something, the driver of the van pulled over to the side of the road. We all got out of the van, and my parents pointed to why we stopped. Stretching across the bright, crystal blue sky between the fluffy white clouds was a triple rainbow. Standing under that brilliant blue sky, gazing at nature's miracle, I didn't know that one day I would be searching for that same sense of wonder, excitement, and adventure, or that I might find it on the tops and sides of mountains. The image of that day is forever imprinted on my mind: the green of the mountains stretching up to touch the bright blue sky and that explosion of color stretching between the clouds.

On the morning of October 9, 1998, Mom, rather than her usual sweats and ponytail that she usually dressed in when we went to the hospital, dressed in her best outfit, fixed her hair, and put on makeup. As Dad lifted me onto the gurney that would wheel me back into the operating room, Mom gently touched my face and said, "Kyle, look at me." I did. As they wheeled the gurney away, I closed my eyes and said through the haze and crushing weight of the anesthesia, "It's okay, Mommy."

Chapter 2

Yes I Can, Sir

From the Halls of Montezuma
To the shores of Tripoli;
We fight our country's battles
In the air, on land and sea;
First to fight for right and freedom
And to keep our honor clean:
We are proud to claim the title
Of United States Marine.

Our flags unfurled to every breeze
From dawn to setting sun;
We have fought in every clime and place
Where we could take a gun;
In the snow of far-off northern lands
And in sunny tropic scenes;
You will find us always on the job
The United States Marines.

Here's health to you and to our corps
Which we are proud to serve;
In many a strife we've fought for life
And never lost our nerve;
If the Army and the Navy
Ever look on heaven's scenes
They will find the streets are guarded
By United States Marines.

The training and teachings of the United States Marine Corps have oozed through my father's veins since the summer of 1984. In 1988, my parents forged a union and founded our family upon what their families' principles — including the Marines — had taught them. Honor, courage, and commitment. Perseverance, fortitude, and trust. The ability to improvise, adapt and overcome the obstacles that presented themselves in life. These would all become guiding principles for me and the rest of my family, especially as we came through my illness and the first few months and years of blindness.

Routine Madness

At age six, laying in a hospital bed, having just had my right eye removed, I wasn't a philosophical protégé. I was a sick, scared, and angry little boy surrounded by family, teachers, and friends, who all wanted me to get better. But I couldn't comprehend that right then. It would take the time and concentrated efforts of my parents and teachers, the words and encouragement of a mentor, and the choices—good and bad—I made over my short lifetime.

And it started when I got home from the hospital.

I knew my house. I ran through its halls and in and out of its rooms hundreds of times, and yet I took tentative steps, reaching out with my hands, unsure of where I was going. I was disoriented, confused, and scared. I didn't want to go outside and shoot hoops. I didn't want to try and Rollerblade or ride a bike. I didn't want to do anything.

So, I did nothing. I sat in my room and cried. I tried listening to books on tape. Sometimes I watched T.V., but for the most part, I sat in my room and felt sorry for myself.

At school, I transferred from Ms. Johnson's regular-ed first-grade class into Mrs. Irving's vision class. Mrs. Irving taught all the visually impaired kids in kindergarten through second grade. I had slowly learned to read and write in Braille as I learned to read and write in print.

I had gone to Mrs. Susan every morning before school started for 30 minutes of Braille lessons throughout kindergarten, and then for the first month of first grade, I would spend part of my day with Mrs. Irving fine-tuning my Braille skills. Now, I was spending all of my class time learning in Braille. This significant change in my schedule, in how

I would learn, threw me off. Nothing was right. Everything was wrong. I wasn't happy, not running around and playing like I used to.

But my parents were not about to let me slide on anything.

After dinner, when it was time to take my plate to the sink, I would stand up and try to leave and just go to my room. I might have gotten away with it once, but the following day when I came back for breakfast, my plate was still sitting there with my unfinished dinner from the night before. "You don't want to finish your dinner for dinner, then you can finish it for breakfast," was a common thing I heard. Once my plate was clean, and if I didn't take it to the sink, Mom or Dad would say, "You know exactly where the sink and dishwasher are, so put your plate away." To which I would respond by going to my room and slamming the door.

Once, when my sisters and I started arguing over what we wanted to watch on T.V., Mom came in and turned it off. Then when we whined and complained, Dad stepped in and bellowed, "OUTSIDE NOW!" Once the three of us were standing on the driveway, Dad said just one word: "Run."

"I can't. I'm blind," I squeaked out, more than a bit afraid.

"You can and will all run until I say it's time to stop. So, can you?" Dad replied.

All we could say was, "Yes, I can, sir." And then we ran around and around the outside of the house. When we passed Dad, he would yell, "FASTER!" and we would run faster. I clung to Cassandra's arm, not wanting to trip over anything. "Pick up your feet!" we heard after the second lap.

Now, it may seem strange that my Dad made his three children run outside in circles as discipline. At the time, I did not like doing it, but I think he was smart. My sisters and I were fighting over the T.V. because we had too much energy, and we were just sitting around on a beautiful Florida afternoon. Making us run burned off that energy, calmed us down, and in the process, we got some exercise. It also sent us a message. I think this is why, compared to other families, we were pretty well-behaved kids. We learned early on that acting up had consequences.

Of course, running around my yard that day, I didn't think that. After what seemed like an eternity, but was only about 15 minutes, Dad finally said we could stop and then sent us to our rooms. Sitting in my room, I cried. I hated being yelled at. I hated not being able to see. I wanted to play and have fun. The being blind thing wasn't fun. My parents could tell that I just wasn't able to be a kid. All the special schooling and preparation could not have prepared them or me for blindness. We were all at a loss.

And that's when the brotherhood of the Marine Corps reared its loyal head.

Always Faithful

Candy Clarke belonged to my Dad's Rotary Club. Her husband, Dan, and my Dad were both former Marines. Dan and Candy had become good friends of our family through the connection of the Marine Corps.

Candy had gone to an event where the speaker was a man named Ed Weihenmayer. Ed was a retired Marine Corps pilot who had served in the Marine Corps and flown 107 night-missions over Vietnam. Ed was also a successful Wall Street and business executive. But of more importance and interest to Candy was that Ed's son, Erik, was blind and a tremendous athlete. Candy got hold of Ed Weihenmayer's contact information and passed it along to my Dad.

Dad got in touch with Ed and told him about our family and the struggles I was going through as a new blind kid. Dad arranged for Ed to come to a Rotary Club meeting and speak about Erik and what he did. Dad also arranged for Mom, the girls, and I to come and hear Ed's talk.

One cool November Wednesday morning, I found myself in a pressed dress shirt and slacks riding in the backseat of our Expedition to an early morning breakfast meeting to hear some man speak about his blind son. I listened to Mr. Weihenmayer, and I didn't believe what I was hearing. Mr. Weihenmayer talked about his son, a rock climber, skydiver, snow skier, cyclist, and runner. He also climbed mountains around the world.

There was no way that this man's son was blind.

After his short talk, Ed met with my family and said that Erik was coming to Jacksonville on a speaking engagement. Ed said that he would arrange for me to meet Erik.

"Does Erik really do all that stuff?" I couldn't help asking Mr. Weihenmayer.

"Of course, he does," Mr. Weihenmayer said in his deep baritone of a voice. "Here, let me show you how I guided him on our first-ever hiking trip." With that, Ed Weihenmayer wrapped his right hand around the back of my neck and started steering me around tables and chairs, singing, "Hup two-three-four, come on sonny boy, pick up those feet and march!" I was laughing. But that little escapade was nothing compared to what would come.

Live Your Life

In January, I met Erik Weihenmayer. Dad picked me up early from school, and I changed into a nice shirt, tie and slacks. We drove across town and arrived just before the end of Erik's speech. When he finished, Erik came and shook my hand. "Hey Kyle, I'm Erik." And then he asked our Dads—who were both standing there—just to let the two of us talk.

Erik and I sat at a table and just talked while our two Marine fathers sat at a table not far away. Often people want to know what Erik said to me. They think there is a magical word or combination of words that sent me from borderline depression to euphoric daredevil ready to conquer the world. The truth of the matter is that Erik and I just talked. Or rather, Erik talked, and I listened. Erik was born with a rare eye disease called retinoschisis. This disease causes the retina to split and detach from the center of the pupil. As Erik grew up, his vision worsened before he finally went totally blind in his early teens. He fought blindness, denying that he was blind. Finally, one day Erik lost his way in the hall at school trying to find the bathroom and needed to ask for help.

Then, one day, Erik was complaining to the driver of a van that carried disabled children. "I don't belong in this car. It's for cripples," Erik said. Finally, the driver got fed up and kicked Erik out of the car. The driver threw a basketball, and it bounced off the side of Erik's head. "You're blind; get used to it." Then he added, "This time, I'm gonna tell you when it's coming, and I want you to put your hands out. Now!" Erik caught it.

Then the driver told him, "Erik, you may not want to be blind, but you are. Let people help you, and you'll learn to help yourself. You might just learn to catch again."

Erik asked me what I liked to do. "I don't know. I can't really do much now. I used to like to play basketball," I said.

"So, did I, but then I learned to do other things," Erik shared. "Don't you rock climb?" I asked him.

"Yes, I do. Have you ever tried it?"

I shook my head. After a short pause, Erik said, "Kyle, I can't see you shake your head."

That made me laugh. I had heard my first blind joke. "No," I said.

"I think you should. I think you'd enjoy it," Erik said. "All you do is feel around on the wall and grab on and pull up. You're a smart kid, and rock climbing is a fun mind game as well as great fun and exercise." We finished by Erik introducing me to his German Shepherd guide-dog, Seego. And then Erik told me, "Kyle, just because you're blind doesn't mean you can't live your life. It's not always easy, but it can be fun, and you will succeed in accomplishing your dreams. Live your life. Can you do that?" "I think I can, sir."

Then we shook hands, and my Dad and I left. I went home thinking a lot about what Erik had said. I was excited. "If he can do that, then maybe I can too," I thought. Erik's story opened my eyes to the many different possibilities in life. There were choices. I didn't fully understand then what I do today, but over time I learned that I could improvise, adapt, and overcome obstacles if I just put my mind to it.

Just like Erik, my independence did not come in leaps and bounds. It took time, baby steps. My parents both expected my sisters and me to give our all-in school and in life. Thus, I began.

Time Will Tell

Before long, a year had gone by, and a family friend, David Bernhardt, suggested to Dad that he and his sons take Dad and me rock climbing at the local climbing gym. Excitement welled up inside me, the thrill of adventure and a sense of wonder that I had not felt since going to Montana before I went totally blind.

The day came, and David pulled me aside. "Kyle, I don't quite know how this is going to work, but I think I've figured out a system."

Being blind is all about developing systems. Systems that work and that are efficient. David Bernhardt's "clock system" for rock climbing would be the first of many systems that I would develop throughout my life. I would use systems in school, my personal life, and especially in the mountains.

The clock system worked like this. David would use my hands and feet as the clock's hands, and the rock wall would be the actual clock face. David would direct me, "right hand to 1 o'clock, left foot out to 9 o'clock. Now stand up and reach with your left hand to high noon." We gave it a shot.

I stood at the wall base, and David helped me put on a massive tangle of nylon loops that made up a climbing harness. The harness wrapped around my waist and both legs. It was not comfortable. Then came the rope. David tied me into the rope using a "figure-eight" knot.

The rope stretched up and secured to the top of the wall. David ran the other end of the rope through a device known as an Air Traffic Controller (ATC). With this, he took up the slack in the rope so that if I fell, it wouldn't be too far.

It was time to climb.

Contrary to popular belief, I was not a naturally born talent on the wall. It's not an easy thing, hauling yourself up a 90-degree vertical wall clinging to rough-hewn holds as if your life depends on it. But David's calm and patient voice guided me up the wall. I fell into a rhythm.

"Right hand 2 o'clock. Left foot to 8:30. Right foot out to 3 o'clock. Stand up and reach high toward 11:30."

I made it to the top of my first climb slowly, but I made it, and that was all that mattered. But there was one small problem. How was I supposed to get down?

David called up to me: "Okay, now put your feet straight out in front of you and sit on the rope." I did what David said. "Now you need to jump, and the rope will hold you as I lower you down."

"Whoa!" I thought, "Hold on a second. I don't know if I trust this." David encouraged me to give it a try. I did. I jumped, and the rope held, but there was one thing I had not counted on: In physics, there are these things called pendulums that, when set in motion, swing back and forth with a continuous motion unless a force like gravity or another force—like a wall—stops them. I was at the end of a pendulum that was about to get stopped. Another interesting fact about physics is that one of the main components of all physics is gravity. When I jumped off that wall, the combination of David lowering me on the rope, my body weight, the force of gravity, and the pendulum-like movement of the rope made my legs feel a little heavy. I did what any novice climber would have done. I let my legs drop. Big mistake! I seemed to have forgotten about the wall—that is until I slammed into it as flat as a pancake. I tried again with David's and my Dad's encouragement, but the same thing happened. This time David told me to just sit in the harness and drag my feet along the wall. I did, and I made it down in one piece.

I was sore and bruised but elated. I had just defied all the natural laws of the world and climbed up a 30-foot wall. I had done what a great many sighted people might not even try, and a tiny seed of determination planted itself inside me. I was eight years old, cancer had not beaten me, and blindness was not about to beat me either.

Meeting Erik Weihenmayer was a turning point in my life. I went from being a scared, angry, and frustrated little boy to someone who could look forward to the future. Erik lit a fire within me, but it was my family—my parents and sisters—that cut the firewood and then laid it in place. And, it would be my family that would tend to and continue to build up that fire within me.

My Dad's Marine Corps background made some growing-up moments a little more boot camp-like. Time and time again, I learned that obstacles and hardships are put in our paths. However, it's what we do with those obstacles and hardships that make us into the people we become.

The first obstacle put in my path was a big one. Meeting Erik and growing up having the parents that I did taught me my first major life lesson—taking my obstacles and hardships and turning them into growth and character-building opportunities. I was learning that I could do anything. I just needed to choose to have an unbreakable and determined mindset.

I may have had eye cancer, but what I was learning to say was, "Yes, I can, sir."

Chapter 3

School Daze

I once had a teacher who said, "I can walk into the door a hundred times. But until I turn the doorknob, it's not going to open." Life is full of closed doors. Some require no more than a gentle push to open. Some require a turn of the knob. And still, others need a key.

Blindness was like the locked door that I kept walking into. Meeting Erik was like being handed the key to unlock the door. Then it was just a matter of turning the knob and walking on through. But blindness wasn't my only closed door. And Erik wasn't the only one with the keys.

My parents certainly had a whole ring of keys to give me, which opened many doors over the years. But one of the more essential keys on that keyring was a key to a toolbox. The toolbox of education.

ABCs

Overall, going to school—learning—as a blind person wasn't easy. At times it was hard. But there's one thing for sure, I learned something from every teacher I had, from preschool through college.

When we moved to Jacksonville, Florida, for my dad's job, I went to Fishweir Elementary. Fishweir was special, not because of its focus on academics or liberal arts programs, but because it had a "Vision Program." Some teachers could teach kids that were blind or had severe visual impairments. The cool thing was that I wasn't the only kid that couldn't see very well.

From the ages of three to six, I wore extremely thick prescription eyeglasses. I'd wonder why my friends didn't have to wear glasses. But at Fishweir, several other kids wore glasses similar to mine.

My preschool teacher, Mrs. Susan, taught me both my print and Braille alphabets. When it came time for kindergarten, my vision was good enough to function in the regular kindergarten class. My parents knew that I had to continue to learn Braille. Every morning, before school started, I'd go to Mrs. Susan's classroom, and she'd continue to work with me on Braille.

Near the end of kindergarten was when school started to become a serious challenge because of my sight. That was because, in February of that year, I had my left eye. Now I was operating with half my field of vision. And it was blurry, unfocused vision. I couldn't see to read our daily writing exercise that was on the chalkboard. My kindergarten teacher had a sheet with large black print made for me to read. The large print made it possible for me to continue my work.

But then the lines on the notebook paper became blurry, and my handwriting sloppy because I couldn't write straight. One day, when I was struggling with the writing exercise, a parent who was helping out that day had a brainstorm. She took my pencil and colored the lines that I was supposed to write on. Suddenly my handwriting was neat and straight again. Slight adjustments and adaptations like that helped me get through kindergarten and a month of first grade.

As I neared the time for the removal of my right eye, even the large print of the teachers' book wasn't enough, and I began relying more and more on Braille. I started spending more time in the K-through-2 vision teacher's room. Mrs. Irving taught all of the kids aged kindergarten through second grade that were legally or totally blind at Fishweir. I transferred to her class full-time after the removal of my eyes.

It was around this time that I met Mrs. Drane, the orientation and mobility specialist. She taught me how to navigate as a blind person. She taught me "sighted guide"—holding onto someone else's wrist or elbow while they led me around obstacles. Then when I went totally blind, she taught me how to use a cane. She showed me how to tap it in front of each foot as I walked, covering just enough space to either side of me to ensure I wouldn't crash into something. And I learned.

Keyboard Navigation

Once I got past the initial shock and anger of blindness, I found myself quite adept at school. I learned quickly and loved a good challenge. I was a talented writer and came up with all kinds of stories to write about in Braille for our daily writing exercises. I was tested for the Gifted Program and accepted, going to a special accelerated class once a week to learn how to push my ingenuity in different ways.

Sometime late in my first-grade year, I was introduced to the computer by another vision teacher at Fishweir, Ms. Dando. Ms. Dando taught the third, fourth, and fifth-grade vision students. Maybe I was a little bit more advanced for my age, or maybe Mrs. Irving, Mrs. Keels (the other vision teacher who helped Mrs. Irving), and Mrs. Drane just saw something in me that made them introduce me to Ms. Dando. She taught me to type on a regular keyboard by knowing where the F and J were and then using different fingers to hit other letters and numbers. We first used a program called "Talking Typer" but soon moved past that to using JAWS for Windows, a fully integrated screen-reading software that would speak the text on the computer screen aloud to me as I used the keys to navigate the computer. I still use JAWS to this day. Today I use it more for searching the Internet, updating my various social media pages, and writing a good portion of this book.

School progressed without incident until my fifth-grade year. In fifth grade, things started changing.

Mainstream Uneasiness

My parents, Ms. Dando, and Mrs. Drane, all sat me down and told me that I would become a mainstream traveling student meaning my only class with Ms. Dando would be math, the most Braille intense subject. In the other subjects, language arts, history, science, etc., I could learn and do my work on the computer. I'd go to the other two mainstream fifth-grade teachers at Fishweir to learn these subjects.

For nearly four years—first through fourth grade—I'd learned alongside vision impaired kids like me. There were less than 15 of us spanning three grade levels. Now I was expected to go into a regular classroom and learn alongside students I barely knew, that barely knew me, and from teachers that didn't have experience teaching a blind kid. There was a transition period. The biggest hurdle for me to clear wasn't academic. It was the social hurdle. In the vision class, I was one of the smartest, most athletic, and confident kids. But around sighted kids who read fast, who didn't stumble or trip when they crossed the classroom, or who could see when the teacher pointed at something she was talking about (like the chalkboard or a picture), I turned into a shy, nervous, and scared kid.

I'd sit in the back of the class, listen, and do my work. I'd go home, go to rock climbing practice, do my homework, and go to bed. When it came time to turn in my homework the next day, I was too shy to feel around on the teacher's desk for the basket where my homework was supposed to go. Or if I did manage to find a basket, it was usually the wrong basket. I was too afraid to ask for help, so I stopped turning in my work. And when the first progress report came out, I had all zeroes.

One of my mainstream teachers, Mrs. Morris, sat down with Ms. Dando and me. She asked me why I hadn't been turning my work in, and I admitted that I was too proud and scared to ask for help. She gave me two options. I could either take the zeroes and risk failing the quarter and thereby risk repeating the fifth grade. Or I could make up all the work I'd missed and turn it in. The catch was, I had one week to do it.

I did the work.

That was my first lesson in self-advocacy. It was a hard one to learn. But from then on, I gained confidence and not only passed but excelled in my classes.

The Search

As the end of fifth grade approached, my parents and I began our search for a middle school. We wanted somewhere that would challenge me academically and athletically. And somewhere where I could grow socially. Our first visit was to the Florida School for the Deaf and Blind in St. Augustine, Florida.

This state-sponsored school offers worlds of opportunity for many blind and visually impaired kids all over the state. As we toured the school, I didn't feel I belonged. While it would be a return to being with kids who understood the challenges of being blind, I was eager and ready to take my place in a sighted world. I'd become good friends with many sighted kids and already felt more comfortable with sighted kids than visually impaired kids. And as my parents had explained to me before, I was eventually going to function in a sighted world. While I respected the students and teachers at FSDB, it wasn't the right fit for me.

We looked at other schools.

In the end, it came down to two schools: Episcopal High School (a private school with grades six through 12) and James Weldon Johnson College Preparatory Middle School (at the time considered the number one academic middle school in the state). I visited both schools, spending a full day at each.

My first visit was to Episcopal. While everyone was polite, the teachers seemed wary of having a blind student. They convinced themselves that I'd be unable to participate in many of the activities and lessons. For example, the day I visited, the science class was dissecting owl pellets. The teacher thought I couldn't handle the tools and wouldn't be able to identify the bones pulled out of the pellets. Therefore, I wouldn't learn. We decided to reserve judgment until we visited James Weldon.

It didn't take a full-day visit at James Weldon to know that it was where I wanted to be for middle school. The teachers taught with enthusiasm and zeal that sucked you in and made you eager to learn.

They didn't assume the all-knowing powerful teacher role but instead embraced the idea that "when one teaches, two learn."

When my parents conferenced with the teachers at James Weldon, they seemed excited at the prospect of having me as a student. Where the teachers at Episcopal saw insurmountable obstacles when it came to teaching a totally blind student, the teachers at James Weldon saw new and exciting opportunities. Not just for me, but themselves. They could find ways to be more creative with their teaching methods, more descriptive in their language, and become better teachers. They wanted me there. They knew that there would be some challenges, but they saw the big picture, and the prospect was too enticing not to pursue.

School Prep

In fall 2003, I became the first totally blind student to attend James Weldon Johnson College Preparatory Middle School. The next three years exposed me to teachers who provided me with tools that would last me a lifetime.

Since I was the only blind student at James Weldon, my IEP (Individualized Education Plan) was extremely important. It outlined that I needed extra time for taking tests, the option to record my classes with a tape recorder, and present my tests and assignments in Braille. The person who helped make this possible was my Vision teacher.

I had three vision teachers while at James Weldon and several throughout my school career. Julie Kronquist, sixth grade; Pat Ree, seventh grade; Susan Kahn, eighth through tenth grade; and Rebecca Allen, eleventh and twelfth grade. All these teachers spent a lot of time transcribing tests and assignments from print to Braille to read and participate in class alongside my fellow students. They also transcribed my assignments from Braille to print so my teachers could grade them.

While I'd been doing much work on the computer in fifth grade, the level and amount of work at James Weldon was to the point that I reverted to using Braille for everything. My schoolwork wound up going through quite a process to get graded. The teachers would turn their class assignments into the vision teacher. She would then work on scanning or typing them into the computer and then running them through a Braille translator and reading through it to double-check and make sure that no translation errors had occurred. Once that was complete, she'd print out (in Braille) the assignment and give it back to the teacher. Then I received the document and read and completed the assignment. I'd then turn it into the teacher, who would then give it back to the vision teacher to be transcribed from Braille into print so the teacher could read and grade it.

Confusing? Sound like a lot of unnecessary work? It was.

I'll admit I probably wasn't the easiest blind student. I had the knowledge and ability to do more stuff on the computer, but being in the classroom, interacting with my classmates was very important to me. I could have left the classroom to go to the guidance office where I had a computer with JAWS set up, but then I risked missing the teacher announcing an addition or change to the assignment or the next part of the lesson. One of the things that my vision teachers and I worked on was trying to make our process more efficient.

In eighth grade, Mrs. Kahn and I made a bet on the University of Florida versus Florida State University football game. (I was a Gator fan, and Mrs. Kahn was an FSU graduate and fan). If the Gators won, Mrs. Kahn would arrange a meeting with a technology representative from a company that sold the latest and greatest technology for the blind and visually impaired, including the latest portable electronic note-takers, which had the potential to replace my Brailler. If I lost the bet and FSU won the game, I'd have to wear an FSU T-shirt. (The Gators won.)

But until that bet went down, I'd carry my heavy Brailler—a machine that looks a lot like a typewriter—from class to class. With my Brailler in my left hand and my long, white cane in my right, I was undoubtedly a force to be reckoned with in the hallway. Often students would hear the tap tap tap of my cane and nearly fall over each other, clearing a path for me so that they wouldn't get accidentally whacked by my aluminum cane or bumped by my heavy-duty Brailler. Some students would try to jump over my cane if they didn't get out of the way in time. Quite often, they'd land on my cane, either bending it severely or simply breaking it. I'm sure my orientation and mobility instructor, Karlin Michelson, got tired of bringing me replacement canes.

I once had a teacher in high school say that my walking down a crowded hallway gave her a good idea of how the parting of the Red Sea might have looked. The smart students walked behind me out of the line of fire.

A+ Teachers

Between threading my way through the hallways and juggling my various assignments and textbooks in Braille—did I mention that a Braille textbook can sometimes span 80 volumes? —here was the real reason I went to James Weldon. The teachers at James Weldon were second to none. I couldn't help but want to learn when they spoke. All my teachers pushed me and taught me something different.

In sixth grade, whether it was my history teacher, Mr. Williams, pushing his student's ingenuity by having us define and explain the meanings of historical vocabulary, dates, and events by not just copying out of the book, or Mr. Weisicki, science, expecting me to know the difference between rocks by touch and chemicals by smell and sound. They helped lay a foundation for my later successes.

In seventh grade, I got to experience first-hand how innovative and creative a teacher can be. My geography teacher, Robert Perry, wasn't sure how he'd teach a blind student geography. How does a blind kid read a map? He searched high and low for suitable Braille or tactile maps, and when he couldn't find any, he decided that he'd make some. He super enlarged several maps of regions worldwide and then traced the borders in puffy paint. My job was to type out Braille labels to place on capitols or other key places on the map.

We had to invent a country for our final project and use all the skills we'd learned throughout the year in its development. While all the other students were drawing maps and charts, Mr. Perry gave me a large piece of cardboard and a few blocks of modeling clay to build a three-dimensional country. Fun accommodations like that made me work that much harder for a teacher. For instance, for my seventh-grade History Fair project, I wanted to do it on Morse Code. But, Mr. Perry gently persuaded me to write a research paper on Braille. I took first place in the research paper category in the school-wide competition, and my paper went on to the Regional Fair.

No Excuses

Something that my teachers did was never excuse me from an assignment. When we dissected owl pellets in Mrs. Welsh's seventh-grade science class, I had to be extremely careful in picking through and separating the tiny delicate bones. On top of being blind and reading and writing in Braille, the lessons themselves were extremely challenging.

All of this was preparing me for later in my life. What I learned at James Weldon was how to enjoy learning, work through problems creatively and how a good teacher can pave the way for your later successes.

High School

For many kids, high school is a fun and exciting time. It's high school sports, dating, staying out late, driving, prom, and all those rights of passage. For me, high school was four years of mind-numbingly hard work. My high school was Paxon School for Advanced Studies—an Academic Magnet college preparatory high school. In a nutshell, we were a bunch of brainiacs taking college courses in high school. Then, if we passed the Advanced Placement (A.P.) test, we'd receive a certain amount of college credit at the end of the course to apply toward our college degrees if we chose to take that route.

During my freshman year, I didn't take any A.P. classes to adapt to high school life. I had a period where I worked with Mrs. Kahn, my vision teacher, on various technology options to use in class to make my learning experience quicker, easier, and more efficient. Once a week during this period, I'd also go with my orientation and mobility teacher, Mrs. Michelson, to various parts of town to work on cane and city travel. I learned how to know when to cross the street safely by using the sound of the traffic as my guide. I learned how to tell direction by the sun, use public transportation, and identify numbering systems—building addresses, rooms inside buildings, and more.

I didn't take A.P. classes my freshman year, but I was still in all Honors classes. While the claim was that they geared the curriculum toward challenging students in all aspects, at the time, I believed that my teachers had nothing better to do than make me miserable by dumping several hours of homework on me every night. The biggest lesson I learned in high school was time management.

Hours In a Day

I'd arrive at school around 8 a.m. Then we would have four classes of 90 minutes each, with a 45-minute lunch. The next day I'd attend my other four classes of 90 minutes each for a total of eight classes alternating days. School was out by 3:15. From October to February, I'd attend wrestling practice from 3:30 to 5:30 p.m., then go home, shower, eat, do my homework, and go to bed. Sometimes I would get to bed around midnight or 1 a.m. I knew I had to work on improving my time management.

I began waking up early to get as much homework done as I could before school. Then I'd use any free time in class, at lunch, or in the car to cut down on the amount of homework time at home and increase my sleep time. This process helped me tremendously in the next three years.

Beginning my sophomore year, I took A.P. classes, learning how to do college-level work. There were times when I felt I wouldn't finish.

And there were times when I felt I was just treading water. But, when that happened, I'd get a good grade, or a teacher would say something that kept me digging deeper. For instance, my chemistry teacher, Mr. Sciullo, always had some kernel of wisdom to pass on. He'd say something like, "There's no path of least resistance." Or,

"There are only two types of people in the world: those that make the Big Mac and those that order the Big Mac. Which will you be?" Or, my personal favorite, "Every day is a holiday, every meal is a feast, and every paycheck's a fortune." We called these "Sciullo-isms," and I'd often write them down and remember them.

Math was always my most challenging subject. When I got to pre-calculus in eleventh grade, my math textbooks often spanned more than 100 volumes, and one pre-calculus math problem could take me multiple sheets of Braille paper. I'd often come in before class—during my lunch period—to start on a test and then come back the next day during lunch to finish it. To save time and paper, I started cutting corners and doing my math in my head.

By my senior year, I was doing all of my schoolwork entirely on my new note-taker—The Braille Note—which I could hook up to a printer and print out my work. I replaced procedural challenges with academic ones. This switch helped me enormously in college when I didn't have a vision teacher transcribing things from print to Braille and back again.

I went on to earn a B.A. in Communication from the University of Central Florida in Orlando in just three years. I owe a lot of that success to my teachers, who constantly challenged me to do better.

All in all, school was hard. I learned a ton, and not all was academic. My teachers showed me how to be creative, intuitive, and analytical. I gained an enormous knowledge base that I draw from every day. Most of all, it ingrained in me a work ethic, which as a blind student I had to have to succeed, that has never left me.

I am fortunate that I received the education that I did. I got to go to the best schools with the best teachers. And that afforded me many more opportunities than a lot of kids. I had teachers go above and beyond the call of duty for me. Some teachers became good friends I know I can still turn to for help when I need it. But even though I'm out of school, I'm never done learning.

Education is one of our most vital tools. Often, it's one of the hardest doors to open, but the reward is that much sweeter for it.

Chapter 4

Rock Jock

I dipped my hands into my chalk bag and listened as Dad described what I was to do while clipped into the rope with the ATC. I was standing at the top of a 100 plus foot cliff in northern Georgia. I was to rappel down to the base and then climb back up.

To my left was another man and his son—Tony and Josh Byott. Josh was a year older than me but a new climber. He'd never done a major rappel like the one that loomed behind us. To me, this was an old hat, but I knew what Josh was going through. The shaky legs, the ringing in the ears, the dizzy head as you looked down that long drop beneath your feet. In my infinite blind wisdom, I decided to give Josh a hand. I told him, "Hey Josh. Just do what I do."

"Yeah...and what's that supposed to be?" he asked, irritated. I grinned, "Don't look down." And very slowly, we inched our way down the cliff. Usually, I would've gone bounding down, but I figured Josh needed some moral support.

Going Vertical

Climbing had opened a whole new world for my family and me. After David Bernhardt took Dad and me climbing, Dad decided that the family needed to get into the sport. So, we got a family membership to the climbing gym. And climbing became a family activity.

Once or twice a week, we'd get together and go to the gym and climb. We even planned to have my ninth birthday party there. But the plans fell through, and instead, my parents took that money and put it toward private climbing lessons for me.

My first ever climbing coach was Thomas Karst—a 17-year-old part-time employee. Thomas was the first of several coaches that would work with me. I was enthusiastic and had tons of boundless energy. But the key was harnessing that energy and making it translate to climbing.

We went to work.

Learning the Ropes

I climbed with Thomas for about an hour once a week after school. He taught me how to strap on my harness and then tie a figure-eight knot thoroughly enough that I could do it in my sleep. He showed me stretches and exercises that would strengthen up my fingers and forearms. Thomas taught me the special climbing lingo.

I learned about the different types of climbing. Bouldering was a short, challenging climb done low to the ground with no ropes and required powerful moves. Top rope climbing was where the climber tied into the rope secured to the top of the wall using a figure-eight knot, then hung down and was held and controlled by a second climber. This second climber ran the rope through a device known as an ATC, which, using friction, would allow them to take up slack in the rope while the climber climbed.

I learned about lead climbing, where the climber tied into the rope and then climbed up the wall—with the rope hanging beneath him—clipping it into quickdraws attached to metal rings screwed into the wall. It's the lead climber's responsibility to secure the rope to the top of the wall so that others can top rope the climb. I would later learn that volunteering to lead climb is also known as "taking the sharp end of the rope."

After taking lessons with Thomas for a couple of months, I joined "Rock Lizards," —a program that met twice a week for young kid rock climbers. Now I was climbing with kids my age. My sisters joined Rock Lizards as well, and pretty soon, the gym manager and Thomas' dad—Tom Karst—talked to my parents about signing my sisters and me up for the newly formed competitive climbing team.

At age 10, I found myself attending rock climbing practices three times a week for two to five hours at a time.

A blind competitive rock climber is probably similar to a European football team playing in the Super Bowl, or—as Erik Weihenmayer might say—"Like a Jamaican bobsledder." To my knowledge, there hadn't been a blind competitive rock climber—at least in the United States—until I decided to crash the party. At first, the USCCA (United States Competitive Climbing Association—now USA Climbing) was resistant. "There's no way he'll be able to stay en route. And if he can't stay en route, then he'll be disqualified."

But my parents and coaches pointed out to the USCCA officials that we had a system of guiding me up the wall. The clock system had been working beautifully ever since I started climbing. But the officials claimed that it gave me an "unfair advantage" considering that competitors were not allowed to receive beta (helpful information) or coaching while on the climbs.

After some back and forth talks, the USCCA finally relented and realized that this was not an unfair advantage because they only told me where the holds were. But they did have some stipulations. They'd assign a fellow competitor—from a different age division and team—to be the one to call out to me where the holds were. We accepted this and prayed that I wouldn't get sabotaged in any way, shape, or form.

The competition season began. Our first "Comp" was in Melbourne, Florida.

Rules, Routes, and Ratings

Climbing competitions are really unlike many traditional sporting events. There are several different types of competitions. Unless climbers compete in a designated "Speed Climbing Competition," they don't traditionally race each other to the top of the wall. Rock climbs are all given a rating of difficulty. Depending on where in the world you live, these ratings differ greatly. Here in the U.S., we use what's called the Yosemite Decimal System (YDS). This scale runs on a difficulty rating of 5.0 to 5.16. 5.0 to 5.4 are usually no more than an easy scramble up a 45-60 degree slope. A rating of 5.5 to 5.7 is similar to climbing up a ladder. These climbs have big chunky holds that are easy to hold onto, and there's less risk of falling. 5.8-5.9 is where most "weekend climbers" become comfortable. 5.8-5.9 would be considered the beginning of an intermediate realm. Dedicated weekend climbers shoot for 5.10 (pronounced "five-ten"). This level requires a large amount of strength, endurance, and technique. 5.11-5.15 is the realm of the true experts, requiring a great deal of training, natural ability, and repeated working of routes.

In the traditional "Redpoint" competition, each climb receives a rating, and then that rating is removed, and it's assigned a point value. The climber gets a set number of attempts to climb and complete the climb to receive the points. Each climber is given a scorecard and encouraged to climb as many climbs as possible. At the end, they tally the top five climbers, and the climber with the most points is the winner.

There are variations in this format. There are specific "Bouldering" competitions, "Speed" competitions, and there are "Onsight" competitions. Our comp in Melbourne was the traditional "Redpoint" competition.

I met Chris—a climber from the 12-13 age division assigned to talk me up the climbs. He was a nice guy, and we got along great. My coaches, parents, and I explained our clock system, and Chris picked it up quickly.

I climbed to a fifth-place finish at Melbourne in the 11 and Under age division. I then consistently placed in the top six, finishing as high as second place in one comp.

The last competition of the season was the State Championship in Miami. This competition was a different competition style known as an "onsight" competition meaning the climbers could not see the climb before climbing it. Climbers were assigned routes and held in a holding area until it was their turn. Once we tied into the rope to climb, we had five minutes to complete the climb. If we didn't finish in five minutes, we had to come down and continue onto the next climb. If we fell before reaching the top, we had to come down and continue onto the next climb. If we finished before the five-minute time limit, we could use that extra time to study the next climb we were assigned.

I went into the comp confident and ready. And then, the competition officials informed my coach and parents that I would not be allowed to be talked up the wall by Chris or anyone else. They saw it as an unfair advantage since climbers weren't allowed to see the climb until they were right in front of it. They arranged the routes in a way that no routes crossed each other. The officials claimed that I'd be able to find my way up the wall perfectly fine. My parents and coaches were pissed.

I finished my first climb with a little more than a minute to spare. My second climb began well enough. I climbed up and to the right and then seemed to run into a dead end. I felt around on the wall, desperately for a hold. I knew there had to be one just beyond my reach. All the while, I was sweating because I knew the seconds were ticking away. Then I decided to make just a desperate lunge and hopefully grab a hold. I missed—dreadfully—and fell swinging far to the left. My dad later told me that he was struggling as he watched me because there was a hold just beyond my fingertips up and to my left that I could've easily reached if I'd just known where the hold was.

I continued onto my last climb but fell several moves into the climb—again, not knowing where the holds were. I took a disappointing fifth-place given my high expectations. Despite my poor performance, though, I had racked up enough points during the season to be the third-ranked climber in the state in my age division. My sisters, Cassandra, and Kelsey did well—both taking third. Cassandra was the second overall ranked climber in her division, and Kelsey was also the third overall ranked in her division. A couple of weeks later, the USCCA extended invitations to Cassandra and me to travel to Oregon and compete at Nationals.

However, my family had already planned a two-week southeast camping and climbing vacation, so we elected not to go to Nationals.

Hot On The Rocks

That summer, we packed up our car and trailer and drove up to North Carolina. We camped and hiked at several beautiful campgrounds and parks. My sisters and I had a blast at Sliding Rock even though the water was frigid, and the air temperature was in the low 60s. It was chilly.

Of all the campgrounds we stayed in, one sticks out in my family's minds: Davidson River. It'd been raining on and off for a couple of days, and one day, it just started pouring. The rain was so heavy and thick that it was difficult for my sisters to see farther than a few feet in front of them. We were all stuck either in the tents or under the tarp that served as our camp kitchen. Cassandra, Kelsey, and I were all wet, cold, and shivering. Lightning was flashing, and thunder was crashing. Our baby sister, Caitlin, was crying and screaming (she was barely a year old). Dad and Mom decided to pack up the camp and leave to find somewhere less rainy. They told us, kids, to get in the car and wait as they packed up.

Typically, our campsites took a long while to set up and break down. But in the freezing rain, Mom and Dad made record time breaking down, folding up, and packing away tents, tarps, and equipment. Mom went to grab onto a tent pole to break it down and didn't see the giant slug that had made that his hang-out spot. As Mom's hand closed around the slug and pole, the slug exploded, covering her hand in slug guts. Mom was more than a little disgusted and immediately sped to the bathroom to wash her hands.

From Davidson River, we went to Frozenhead State Park—located in Tennessee. We climbed at Obed. We went from wet and rainy weather to blisteringly hot weather.

We were climbing at Image Wall at Obed. It was so hot that Dad and I had to take off our shirts. The sun was baking the granite walls. I attempted to climb a small finger-width crack, but the rock was so hot that I felt as though my fingers were blistering.

After spending a couple of days at Frozenhead and Obed, we drove to northern Georgia. We visited Talula Gorge and hiked down into the gorge, looking at the high monolithic walls and cascading waterfalls. We met up with our friends, the Hendersons, returning to Florida after a climbing trip in West Virginia at the New River Gorge. We camped at Currahee Mountain and spent a couple of days climbing 100 plus foot sandstone cliffs.

It was at Currahee where I probably had the most significant climb of my young climbing career.

It was another epically hot day with temperatures in the high 90s. After a lunch of peanut butter and jelly sandwiches, Dad eyed a climb rated 5.11a. It was about 115-120 feet with an intimidating roof that would require some tricky maneuvering to get over. Then there was a long straight climb with tiny holds all the way to the top. Dad decided to give it a shot and lead it.

He tied in and began climbing while wearing a camelback filled with water that he kept stopping to use. There were points on the climb where he struggled. The rock was so hot, and Dad was sweating so hard and drinking so much water that Mom and Mrs. Henderson joked that they could see the rubber on Dad's climbing shoes melting. He finally finished and set up the rope as a top rope to try and climb.

When he made it down, he said we could try to climb it if we all wanted. But he did say that it was tough and we should just try and climb as far as we could and don't be disappointed if we didn't make it to the top.

I wanted to take a crack at it. I tied into the rope, and Dad told me what to expect. There was a roof about 10 or 15 feet up that I'd need to "pull" to access the straight-up climbing to the very top. I made it up to the roof and reached back, grabbing onto the lip of it. I edged out on it and managed to get my hands up over the edge of the roof to grab onto what felt like a big jug handle. In reality, a beginning climber would have thought it was just a tiny hook that would have been difficult to hang on. But I'd grown as a climber and had been working on my ability to grab extremely tiny holds.

To get over the roof, I had to do one of the worst positions in climbing—a hand-foot match. Typically, you never want to put your hands and feet on the same hold. It takes away much of your strength and power, forcing you to make a risky dynamic move that can throw you off balance and send you toppling backward off the wall—destination terra firma if your partner hasn't got you on a tight belay.

I managed to get one foot up on the lip of the roof and then used my hands to help thrust my body upward. I drove off my right leg and propelled myself up and over the roof. My momentum carried me up. And suddenly I was flying. It felt like I was climbing a 5.5, not a 5.11. Everyone down below was yelling and screaming, "Go, go, go! You're doing it!" I didn't stop; I kept on going until there wasn't anywhere else to go.

I'd just "flashed" a 5.11 in under five minutes. I couldn't believe it.

When I got down, everyone patted me on the back. Dad grabbed me up in a giant bearhug. "You kicked its ass Big Coon," he said.

Then Kelsey stepped up and flashed it too. Cassandra got halfway up but burned out and needed to come down. Kelsey and I were both sky high after flashing our first 5.11. Neither of us could wipe the ear-to-ear grins that spread across our faces.

That night we all went into the little town not far from Currahee Mountain for root beer floats and pizza. It was Mr. Henderson's birthday. And when we got back to camp, Dad made his best Donald Duck impression and sang happy birthday while we all laughed hysterically.

We spent a few more days climbing and hiking but eventually had to get back home.

Rapping Down

When we got back to the gym, I felt like a different climber. I was stronger and doing more challenging climbs. But once the school year started, I began to fade. I couldn't get into the gym as much because school took up much of my time.

One of my teammates, Danny Poor, surpassed me in the overall climbing rankings and demolished me in competitions. The only person I seemed to be better than was our rooky climber—Josh Byott. My second competitive climbing season was a struggle. I just tried to do the best I could. I knew that's all Mom and Dad wanted, but I was used to finishing at the top of the rankings, not the bottom.

After an unimpressive second season—during which I didn't even go to state because of other previous commitments—I was determined to get back in the gym and climb until I was the best. I was a good but not a great climber, and I wanted to be the best.

I was starting to lead climb more and more and able to lead on 5.9 in the gym. I was climbing 5.10 and 5.11 with regularity on top rope and was even starting to take shots on 5.12. But I was also falling out with competitive climbing.

Before starting my third season, I was lead climbing on an overhanging 5.9 when I took a "whipper"—a violent swinging fall—of about ten-fifteen feet. I had taken whippers before, and I knew that it could happen to the best of climbers. I was doing a pull-up with my left hand while my right hand held a quickdraw to clip into the bolt that was just above the overhang. I clipped in but then had to reach down, grab the rope, and pull it back up to clip through the other end of the quickdraw. My left hand gave out, and I fell crying out, "Take, take," to tell my Dad to take up the slack in the rope preventing me from falling farther than necessary. My last quickdraw placement was about five or six feet down. Add some rope stretch and my fall was a little longer than 10 feet.

I'd fallen from greater heights when bouldering or when I'd practiced taking whippers when Thomas Karst was teaching me to lead. This time though, the rope got tangled around my leg, and I had a bad rope burn across my right thigh. I bashed my knees into the wall as the rope arrested my fall. Dad lowered me to the ground, and I untied from the rope and walked away tired, frustrated, and angry after a long day of climbing.

As the new school year approached, Mom and Dad decided that it would be better for us kids to concentrate on school more and made the executive decision to stop climbing competitively. It was frustrating. I dreamed about climbing in competitions. But soon, those dreams faded to be replaced by me climbing intricate, lone pieces of rock with a few partners. I enjoyed the outdoor climbing world much more than the competitive one. I loved competition, but I didn't want always to be known as just "the blind competitive climber."

Throughout my life, I've learned about challenges and adversity and how it defines, makes, and molds us into the people we become. Looking at my life as a whole, you could say that my life was following along a path very much like a rough, rocky mountain trail. When I was born, my parents were sky high and excited about growing their family. Then I was diagnosed with cancer, and we had a long uphill battle. Then we ran into a steep and seemingly impenetrable wall with blindness. You sit and look at it. You don't know how to get around it. Then I met Erik Weihenmayer and was shown how to climb straight up and over that obstacle—taking it head-on. Then the going gets a little easier, and the view is prettier with lush greenery. Being at the top of the competitive climbing rankings and rock climbing and hiking around the Southeast with my family were extraordinary times in my life. It was my first mini peak—or summit. But something I was about to learn was that there's always one just a little higher whenever you reach the top of one peak. And once we become aware of that next peak, we're presented with a choice to try and reach for that next peak, to turn aside, or just to stay put. My parents taught me from an early age not to settle but rather to reach and accept the challenges presented along the way to the top.

When I say that my second competitive climbing season was a struggle and I was falling out of competitive climbing, I realize that it was merely a challenge and a way of preparing me for the challenges ahead. When we got out of competitive climbing, I was pumped, but truthfully it was a transition period as I worked toward my next peak.

Chapter 5

Global Explorers

The Super Inca Trail Tale Begins: June 2006

"I'm the only one wearing a cowboy hat here," Justin said. "I brought my barf-bag," said Terry.

"Oh, is that still recording?" Justin asked in mock horror.

We were standing in the long line for customs at the airport in Lima, Peru. I recorded our conversation on my handheld digital recorder that I had purchased to act as my journal. I'd been looking forward to this day for nearly a year and a half.

During my seventh-grade year, Ed Weihenmayer had passed along some information about a program that he was putting together with a nonprofit organization—Global Explorers. Erik wanted to partner blind and sighted students from across the U.S. and take them on a hiking trip. In honor of Erik's first international hiking trip to Peru when he was in college, he selected Machu Picchu as the destination. Rather than the standard Inca Trail, however, the group would hike the Ankascocha, or the "Super Inca," Trail. The days would be longer and harder, and the team would climb over higher mountain passes. The Program was known as "Leading the Way." I thought it sounded cool and an experience of a lifetime. So, I applied and was selected to be a member of the inaugural Leading the Way Expedition.

In honor of the "Super Inca Trail," we participants were christened "Supers." The program involved monthly conference calls with the other team members, learning about the culture and the environment. We had long lengthy discussions about blindness, leadership, teamwork, community service, and many other topics.

In March 2006, during my eighth-grade year, Global Explorers arranged for us to all fly to Colorado for a weekend retreat to meet everyone for the first time. We had talked over the phone, chatted through the online list-serve and email. But there is something different about actually meeting people in person.

They stuffed the weekend with team-building activities. We all flew into Denver, Colorado, and then drove to Estes Park. We set up shop in the YMCA and prepared for a packed weekend.

The following morning, several of us got up for an early 6 a.m. run. To do so, though, I had set my watch for 5:45 a.m. At the time, my talking watch's alarm was a rooster crowing. When it went off, I heard Justin grumble into the pillow, "I thought I was in Colorado, not back on the farm."

After breakfast, we discussed several different worksheets. Some were on leadership, some discussed environmental issues, and still, another talked about community service.

Blind leading the blind

To work on gaining one another's trust, Erik Weihenmayer and a few of his climbing partners, Eric Alexander and Ben Witherell, set up an obstacle course. A sighted Super would guide a blind Super, using only voice commands, through the course. Then, to spice it up a bit, the blind Super would guide the sighted Super through the course. The course consisted of sighted people making noises to guide us as we walked along. The sighted Supers closed their eyes and held onto the blind Super's shoulders. Then, we would guide them through. I guided Justin "Tex" Grant—flawlessly, I might add—although his cowboy hat getting knocked off as we ducked under the limbo bar might count against me. Justin was from Texas and was rarely without his cowboy hat. And even though he was visually impaired, he still had decent enough vision to where he could occasionally guide a totally blind Super around.

After the obstacle course and lunch, we went for a hike in Rocky Mountain National Park.

Now might be a good time to describe how a blind person hikes. As I have said before, being blind is all about developing systems. When Erik started climbing big mountains in the early to mid-90s, he discovered Leki Trekking Poles. These poles helped give him stability and the ability to scan the trail for rocks, roots, and other obstacles.

Erik's climbing partners would then walk in front of him with bells hanging from the wrist loops of their trekking poles and/or from their backpacks. They would then give verbal directions. The basic "left," "right," "step up," "step down" can sometimes get boring. Erik, Eric, and Ben encouraged us to develop our own "hiking lingo."

Ben explained, "Erik and I sometimes use the names of different things to describe the size of a rock. I'll say 'chickenhead,' and he'll know that it's a smaller-sized rock. Or I'll say 'ankle burners,' and he'll know there are a series of rocks about ankle high. Or I'll say, 'head banger' meaning a tree branch that can hit him in the head."

We blind Supers adopted many of these same systems.

Blazing a Trail

For the first few miles, Brad Jaffke was my guide. Brad was sighted and from Chicago. Occasionally Brad and I would get into a groove, and Brad would glance back and notice that the rest of the group was fading away behind us. "Whoa, slow it up there, K Coon," he'd say. And we would slow down to let everyone catch back up.

We—as a group—would periodically stop to talk. And the sighted Supers would describe our surroundings. They described the transition from rock and snow to green trees and grass.

Erik would remind us all, sighted and blind alike, to reach down and pick up a rock, to touch the trunk of a tree, or to close our eyes and take deep inhales of the crisp Colorado spring air.

That evening we discussed different things we had felt during the hike, and we went through a day-by-day account of what we would do on the Super Inca Trail and where we would go, and the places we would visit while in Peru.

The following day, we reluctantly parted, looking forward to Peru more than ever.

And now the day was here.

Travel Team

We were a large and motley crew. We Supers ranged in age from fourteen to eighteen. Each of us came from a different background. Sighted or sight impaired, we each had our own stories and barriers to breakthrough.

 Alysha Jeans: totally blind from birth from Kansas.
 Andrew Johnson: totally blind from birth from Connecticut.
 Anna Berberet: sighted from Wisconsin.
 Arielle Edwards: visually impaired due to Stargartz disease (a form of macular degeneration) from Oklahoma.
 Brad Jaffke: sighted, from Illinois.
 Charlotte Dawson: sighted from Virginia.
 Cole Loughery: sighted from Illinois.
 Elise Post: sighted from California.
 Estey Masten: sighted from Missouri.
 Jill Millkey: sighted from Georgia.
 Justin "Tex" Grant: visually impaired due to Stargartz Disease (a form of macular degeneration) from Texas.
 Kyle "KB" Bradley: visually impaired due to retinoschisis from Missouri.
 Max Lowe: sighted from Montana.
 Paul Jenkins: totally blind since birth from Virginia.
 Ryan Charlston: sighted from Missouri.
 Terry Garrett: totally blind due to build-up scar tissue after 22 eye surgeries, from Colorado.
 Tiffany Priddy: visually impaired from Oklahoma.
 In addition, we also had Global Explorers representatives Dave Shurna, GEx Executive Director, and Casey Fagre.

 Throw in two camera crews. Phil and Russ would be creating two TV pieces. The first one for ABC World News' person of the week, which would be Erik Weihenmayer. It aired in June 2006. The second would be for ABC Nightline about the trip as a whole. It aired in mid-July 2006.

Bernd, Sebastian, and Mariska were from the Netherlands and studying at the New York Film Academy. They were creating a documentary on our trek, which would come to be known as "Fellowship of the Andes."

Oh, and there were the chiseled and grizzled world-class badasses: Erik "Big E" Weihenmayer, Eric "Erie" Alexander, Jeff "Jefe" Evans and Didrik "D Money" Johnck.

We had a large group. Getting through customs took a while.

Eventually, I made it up to the man checking passports and doing all the paperwork. I handed over my passport, he stamped it, and I moved on. We went to baggage claim, found our checked luggage, and went outside. It was pretty humid and muggy—a bit like Florida. We had a bus that took us to our hotel in a suburb of Lima.

When we arrived, we were assigned roommates. I was in a room with Cole and KB on the top floor of the hotel. We climbed up six or seven flights of stairs and immediately collapsed into bed. It wasn't long after I fell asleep that I was awakened by the phone ringing off the hook and someone pounding at the door.

We arrived at the hotel around 1 a.m. and expected to be up, ready, and in the lobby by 4:30 a.m. Dave would probably be giving us a wake-up call—just in case. In falling asleep, we almost overslept. It was 4:25 a.m. None of us had heard our alarms, the wake-up call, and no one could get into the room to shake us out of it since we had locked all three locks on the door. As soon as we all finally woke up, we lept into our clothes and ran downstairs to make it back to the airport in time for our flight to Cusco.

Dave and Casey told us that Peruvian lines were not as fast as American lines. We needed to be there a little earlier than we usually would have to be at a U.S. airport. I figured there were not any lines slower than those in the U.S. I was sadly mistaken. We stood still for about 30 minutes and then took two steps forward.

Eventually, though, we made it through all the lines, survived an hour flight delay, and finally boarded the plane. An hour after takeoff, we descended into the old Inca capital of Cusco.

Chapter 6

Cusco, Peru

Elevation: 10,500 feet

Walking into the main entrance of the Cusco airport, I heard a live band playing off to the side. Live bands would become a regular part of being in Cusco. They were in restaurants and on street corners.

A breeze softly blew as we loaded up the bus. On the ride to our hotel, Justin, in his way, did his best to describe the city to me, saying, "Everything is like, all Spanish here. All the buildings and stuff—even the grass—reminds me of Texas a little bit."

We reached our hotel and received roommates and room assignments. I was rooming with Brad. We had just enough time to put our luggage in our rooms before our official tour of the city began. Our guide Julio was funny and entertaining. He spoke relatively good English—although now and then, he would break off and search for the right word or would repeat himself. A classic line of his would become, "A very especial place." Everywhere we'd go, he would say, "This is a very especial temple," or "These stones are very especial," or "These were very especial people." We would later joke, saying, "This is a very especial park bench."

After a lunch buffet at a restaurant down the street, where we rocked out to a great Peruvian band while eating, we climbed onto our handy-dandy bus, and Julio took the floor. "We are going to be visiting some very especial places today. First, we are going to visit the Incan ruin of Sacsayhuamán -sak-say-wuh-ho-mahn. Later we will visit the Main Cathedral, which was built by the Spanish, and then maybe, one or two more places."

We were off, driving 20 to 30 minutes up a twisty, bumpy road above the city. Sacsayhuamán was monstrous.

"Some of these stone blocks are about 100 tons," Julio told us. "The Incas did not have any wheeled devices. So, the slaves and the soldiers would all come around and pick up the stone. They would all carry this stone for miles above their heads until they reached this spot. And then they would place it."

"Now what makes the Incas so famous is that they did not use mortar, or clay, or cement. So, when you touch the stones, feel in the cracks to see how the stones fit so well together. So, come and feel the energy in the stones."

The temple walls were monstrous. Laying my hands on the stone, I knew there was no real energetic shock that would pass through the stones and into my hands. But I knew what Julio meant as I touched the wall and felt the roughness under my fingertips. I traced some of the lines and patterns in the rock. I tried to squeeze a finger into the cracks between each stone. It was impossible. They fit together perfectly. And I wondered at and appreciated the work of the Inca people.

Julio told us about the Peruvian culture. He told us about the "Sun Festival" held every year at Saqsayhuman on June 21, the winter solstice, which was the most important day of the year to the Inca. He explained that the Incas were forbidden to climb to the tops of the mountains since they believed the gods lived atop them. And finally, Julio led us up a long series of rough rock-hewn stairs, leading up between the temple walls and onto its top.

The world opened up. And we gazed out over the entire city of Cusco, which was nestled in a valley, surrounded by high mountain peaks. Perched at 11,500 feet, standing atop an Incan temple, I felt something within. A sense of wonder, excitement, and adventure was growing from a fire to an inferno.

After coming down from Saqsayhuman, we visited several other popular sites in Cusco. The Main Cathedral, which was built by the Spanish to try and convert the Inca people to Christianity, was tall and ornately decorated. Walking through its echoing halls, we could not help but feel a deep respect and appreciation for the artwork hanging on the walls and the time and effort needed to build and maintain such a beautiful structure. But despite the beauty of the Cathedral and other sites in Cusco, we were all itching and eager to set out on the path toward Machu Picchu. First up, a trip the next day to the famous Pisac Market and Inca ruin of Ollantaytambo.

Talk, Shop, and Test Treks

The next day started with a little inspirational talk from Erik. I knew Erik's story, having read his book countless times. But all the same, I intently listened as he told us about his first attempts at hiking.

"I didn't really know how to hike. My Dad would twist his hand up in my shirt and drive me down the trail. Sometimes I'd trip over a rock and go flying off the trail. Since his hand was twisted up in my shirt, he'd go flying off the trail with me. He'd be bouncing along on his belly, holding onto me with one hand and holding his little video camera up in the air with his other hand. So by the end of the day, we'd be pretty frustrated with each other. But I'd say to him, "Dad, I'm sorry I got frustrated with you." And he'd say, "It's okay." Then we'd go out the next morning and do it all over again."

He told us about meeting Jeff, Eric, and Didrik through various friends. Together Jeff and Erik had climbed several mountains—McKinley, Aconcagua, El Capitan. Eric Alexander was a big-time skier and guided Erik W, on skis, down the tallest mountains in Europe and Australia. Erik W and Didrik met because Didrik was the teammate on their Everest expedition who sent trip dispatches from Everest to the Internet so people across the world could follow their adventure. (Didrik was doing the same for our trip in Peru.)

Erik talked about surrounding himself with teammates that he could trust enough that he could put his life in their hands and that they could trust him enough to put their lives in his hands. He also challenged us not to be fixated on getting from point A to point B.

"Slow down and enjoy the trip," he told us. "Some of you may be pushing yourselves a little bit, and some of you may be slowing down a bit as well. We should all move slowly since we're getting into higher elevation. But remember that it's not a race into camp. Some of the most fun you'll have is actually on the trail. I remember one time when a friend and I went from the top of one side of the Grand Canyon to the other rim and back in 24 hours. And afterwards, we came across a ranger, and we told her what we'd done. She said, "Would you race through the Smithsonian Institute?" I thought, "Well, no." And she said, "Then why would you race through the Grand Canyon?" I think that's something we should all think about. Slow down and enjoy ourselves. We're traveling through the Smithsonian Institute."

Erik's words and advice would be in the back of my head for the entire trip. But it would take some time to fully understand what he meant about teamwork and enjoying ourselves along the trail. After all, we were here to hike a trail and see some wondrous sites.

After Erik's talk, we drove from our hotel to the Urubamba or Sacred Valley. We stood at a lookout point next to the road, surrounded by locals attempting to sell us various handicrafts, and gazed out over the valley. It looked like a checkerboard of greens and browns surrounded by high mountains. Of course, that is how the sighted Supers described it to me, and I could imagine it quite well. The valley is still used today for growing many crops, such as 25 different types of corn and potatoes. (As a side note: Many people are not aware that Peru is the potato capital of the world. There are over 370 different varieties of potatoes grown all over Peru, including the Urubamba Valley.)

We eventually made it to the town of Pisac and strolled through the market. Many of us bought alpaca-wool sweaters, blankets, or hats, as well as a variety of musical instruments and other handicrafts. I also took a stroll, with Eric Alexander, through the food section of the market. Eric described to me the various food items for sale. There were fruits, vegetables, and carcasses of various meats, among other things. We watched a woman loading her food purchases onto a blanket and then wrapping the blanket around herself, tying the four corners of the blanket together in front of her, making a little backpack.

Then it was back to the bus, off to lunch, and then to the ruin of Ollantaytambo.

Ollantaytambo, named after a famous Inca warrior, was a series of 15 terraces linked by rough rock steps leading up the mountainside. We climbed to the top of the ruin and again looked down at Ollantaytambo on one side and the Urubamba River on the other.

We descended back to our bus and drove back to our hotel. Even with it being a long and full day, we had many more ahead of us.

Thought-Provoking

Our third full day in Peru started much like the second day had. Except this time, it was Eric Alexander's turn to tell us about his life, views on leadership and to inspire us to work as a team.

Eric A and Erik W met through a mutual skier friend. One night, Erik W crashed on Eric A's couch, and they got to talking about climbing.

"He was blind," Eric told us, "And I thought, 'Oh, that's cute. He probably means hiking. He probably doesn't know what he's talking about.'

"I'd skied with people who were blind before, so I knew what they were capable of on the ski slope. But climbing that was a whole 'nother story."

The pair spent a day climbing frozen waterfalls. They kept pushing the limits climbing harder and more dangerous routes until Eric A realized that Erik W had something special and the two of them were going to have a lot of fun in the mountains together.

They went on to climb several mountains together. Erik W invited Eric A to be a member of the Everest expedition. But Eric A came close to missing out not only on the expedition but also on the rest of his life.

On a training climb called Ama Dablam—a steep, dangerous, but beautiful Himalayan peak—Eric A was climbing down from one camp to the next. He stepped on a large loose rock which tipped over and slid over a 600-foot cliff taking Eric A with it. Fortunately, it wasn't a straight vertical drop, allowing Eric A got to bounce his way down, and by some miracle, he landed on his feet on a small ledge.

"It was about the size of a chair. Luckily, I landed on my feet. Didn't break any bones! It was one of those moments when you think, "Am I dead?"

After Eric A climbed back up and crawled into his tent, he woke in the middle of the night with a gurgling in his lungs. He had contracted high altitude pulmonary edema—a deadly altitude sickness that fills the lungs with fluid and puts the climber in danger of drowning in his lungs. The quickest remedy for the condition is immediate descent to lower altitude. With the help of teammates, Eric A made it down to base camp and evacuated by helicopter to a hospital in Kathmandu. "The weather was bad, and the helicopter managed to land for just a minute. I got in, and it took off. As soon as we did, the sky closed up again."

As he got better, Eric A learned even more about being a strong team member. He thought the team wouldn't want him back. The doctor medically cleared him to go to Everest, but doubts crowded his mind. Why would the team want a climber susceptible to pulmonary edema, a potential weak link? Ultimately, it would be Erik W's decision. And when Eric A asked Erik W if he still wanted him on the team, Erik W said, "Being blind my whole life, people have made judgments of what I can and can't do. I'm not about to do that same thing to you."

Erik W's words and faith in Eric A made him realize something. "We all have strengths, but not all in the same area. We need to maximize those for the good of the team. And one of those greatest strengths is our attitude and how we look at and solve problems. And I realized what our goal was. It was to get Erik W to the top of Everest. And I felt that even if I wasn't strong enough to get myself to the top, maybe I could be strong enough to help get Erik W there."

Eric's talk made me wonder if I had the character and the humility to focus not on myself but on something greater. A team working along a trail toward a common goal. A team—step by step—taking a journey together.

Baptism by Fire

After Eric spoke to us, we loaded up the bus with our duffels and backpacks. We wouldn't see Cusco for another week as we would be camping at the trailhead that night and starting the actual hike in the morning. The excitement was so palpable that you could practically taste it.

We still had a couple of other places to visit before we could hit the trail, though: First stop was Moray.

Moray was an experimental agricultural site of the Incas. When we got off the bus, we stood at the lip of what seemed to be an amphitheater. It was a natural hole in the ground. Julio said that archaeologists and geologists alike presume a meteor striking the ground around 150 million years ago created the pit. The Incas used the hole to make perfectly circular terraces. These terraces went down into the hole like giant stairs. The bottom was about 500 feet below us.

We partnered up and headed down into the pit.

We walked across the first terrace. I could feel dry grass and weeds rippling under my feet and trekking poles as I followed Justin to the first of the "floating steps"—as Julio called them. Then Jeff stopped and gathered us all around. He wanted to show the sighted guides how to guide their blind partners down these floating steps. "I want you all to picture what these look like. These stones are anchored into the walls, and that's all that's supporting them. Nothing else. It's just the wall. These rocks are protruding about 16 inches from the wall—like a plank. What you're going to do is walk down these. It's like a little staircase. You need to be careful, though, because there're gaps between the stones. What I want to do here is show you how to get down these using proper technique. I'm going to guide Erik down, and you guys are going to watch and then guide your partners down these steps. Now just so that you are aware—because we always need to be aware of consequences—there's about a six to seven-foot drop on one side. We're going to have somebody there to catch you if you fall, but it's kind of like the three rules in ice-climbing: Don't fall, don't fall, and don't fall. Let's follow those here. So now I want you to listen—and guides watch what I do with Erik's poles. This is how we got Erik through the icefall on Everest time and time again. Verbal cues and then pole placement. Now, I'm going to overextend it with Erik here because he doesn't need this as much. But I want to show you, so you know how to do it."

Then Erik said, "You know, if it came down to it, I don't really need any of his stinking help."

We all cracked up. And in my head, I immediately got a picture of Jeff holding onto Erik's poles, getting ready to place them on a rock, and then Jeff suddenly throwing the poles away from him and leaping across the rocks on his own, calling over his shoulder as he went, "Okay, super blind. Let's see how you do." I smiled to myself at the mental image.

Of course, I'm not really sure exactly how Jeff looked or what he did after Erik said that. But, as we all were laughing, Erik made a pleading voice. "No, no, I'm just kidding! It's for the camera!" (Do we have a comedian in the house?)

"Ok. Here we go," Jeff said. "The idea behind this is teamwork, right?" (I assumed those comments were toward Erik—and us.)

Then Didrik called out to Erik, "Hey, don't start showing off." We laughed again. I smiled to myself again, thinking of how all these climbing friends, brothers, partners, teammates were with each other. I wondered if that was what we, as the Supers, were becoming. I really admired and enjoyed how Erik, Eric, Jeff, and Didrik worked together. They played jokes on each other. They messed around a lot. But overall, they kept each other safe, and they worked well as a team. Maybe this teamwork thing was starting to make a bit more sense.

Justin and I moved to the first of the steps. Stepping down onto the first stone, Justin took my poles and placed them on the stone. Putting my weight on the poles, I lowered one foot, and then the other, onto the rock. Justin stepped down to the next stone, and we repeated the process. But this time, I put my poles in my left hand and placed my right hand on the wall to use as a guide. We did this down the three or four stone steps to the next terrace. Then we walked across the terrace to the next set of stairs and did it all over again.

We climbed down many steps right to the bottom of the hole. We stood in the middle of Moray with the terraces rising steadily up on every side. It was amazing.

When we had all congregated in the middle of Moray, Julio explained that each terrace would have crops going all the way around. The Incas used this site to see what would grow at these elevations, water the crops, and make the most out of them. Then it was time to switch up partners and head up for lunch.

Salt of the Earth

We drove to the Salt Mines of Moras. These were a series of deep saltwater pools from which the Inca would draw salt. The mines are still in use today.

Julio offered around a block of pure salt, which each of us sampled. (And if you're curious—a pinch of pure salt is highly salty. My mouth tasted like salt for the next half an hour or so.)

We walked down a long flight of steps right down amongst the pools. We walked along tight paths varying in width from 15 to 30 inches. There would often be a drop-off, ranging in size from 10 to 30 feet, into a pool on one or both sides. Along one twenty-inch-wide stretch, we had a drop of about fifteen feet into a pool on our right and a tiny stream of saltwater on our left. Cole was guiding me. Erik was hiking right behind me. And Max was behind Erik. I had to put one foot in front of the other and position my weight evenly over each foot. Erik and I had a little competition, which blind guy could step in the stream of saltwater—to the left—the fewest number of times. When we reached a rest spot between some high rock walls, I had stepped in the stream three times, whereas Erik had stepped in it four. (Take that Big E!)

We eventually hiked uphill, crossed a rickety wooden bridge that swayed in the wind, and then arrived back at the bus. We drove to our campsite, unloaded, ate dinner, and got ready for bed. Everyone filled up a water bottle with hot water. Every night the temperature would get down around freezing. We stuck the hot water bottles down in our sleeping bags, which helped keep us warm.

As I lay in the dark of the tent I was sharing with Brad, I thought about all the days, weeks, and months I'd spent preparing physically and mentally for this trip. I was having the time of my life. The weather was beautiful, the hiking was great, and the people were awesome. I smiled, rolled over, and went to sleep.

Chapter 7

The Inca Trail

We woke up to a porter tapping on our tent pole, asking, "hot watty or coca tea?" Coca leaf tea was fast becoming a staple of our regular diet. Contrary to popular belief, it's non-narcotic and quite delicious. It is known to help lessen or negate the symptoms of altitude sickness—primarily headaches. We were highly encouraged to drink the delicious beverage. And if while on the trail we started getting a headache, rather than taking Advil or another drug, we immediately bummed some coca leaves off our guides or porters and chewed them. While on the trail, horses carried our big duffels while being led by porters, who were also our cooks. The porters carried our bags, set up our tents, cooked our meals, and showed us nothing but kindness and respect. Talk about first-class service. Hector and Flaveo were our porters that would come around each morning to our tents to offer a
good-morning beverage of either hot cocoa (hot watty) or coca tea.

Finally, after breakfast, we turned our sights to the trailhead. The trailhead was at about 9,500 feet of elevation. The plan was to follow the trail up to about 12,500 feet before going back down to around 11,500 feet. We would camp on the Chilipahua community school's soccer field.

Thus, we set out moving slowly and deliberately along the trail with rocks scattered along the path. To our left, a steep slope went up to a wall of rocks. As we moved upward, the ground sloped off to our right—every other step held at least five pictures. Justin kept wanting to stop and pull out his camera and take picture after picture. Every so often, when he did this, I would stop and listen to the sounds around me. I could hear the solidness of earth and rock to my left and see the openness of the sky stretching endlessly above to my right.

At the base of the mountain, I heard the roaring and rushing of the Urubamba river. I imagined it—a brutal, untamed giant tearing through the valleys of Peru, carving out its place in history.

Sometimes Justin stopped and described what he was seeing. "At the bottom of the mountain, there seems to be some farmland and a river. There's a road—which I guess we drove down on our way here. Blue skies, a few clouds, and a great view."

Dave Shurna also described a particular landmark. "Off to the right, we have a deep valley—the same valley we've been following all along. Just ahead of us, and to the left, is a long wall. It's probably 15 feet tall and made of small bricks. It almost seems to be holding up the rest of the mountain. There's mountain above it and mountain below it. At the very top of the mountain straight in front of us, there's a series of walls as well. The biggest and longest wall extends probably a few city blocks. So it's a pretty big wall."

Death Falls

It is truly amazing getting to see the world and trail through the eyes of other people. However, it can be a little disconcerting when you're hiking along a mountainside with a 2,000 to 3,000-foot drop on one side. You're hiking along, and your partner casually throws out, "Oh yeah, if you fall, make sure to fall to the left. Because if you fall to the right, you'll probably die." We classified potential falls in three different ways. "Death" meant if you fell, you would probably die. "Severely pissed off" meant a fall that could result in a trip to the hospital. (The attempt to classify these as "hospital falls" failed epically.) And finally, there were the falls that would make you "mildly annoyed."

Justin particularly enjoyed describing death falls to me. "As you left the mountainside, there would be a nice feathery feeling of leaves and tiny plants rustling past your skin. Then you would be met by thorns which would puncture you probably about an inch deep all over your body. Then you'd come in contact with some rocks and bounce a few times before becoming airborne. And if you are not already dead, you will certainly die as you fall and are splattered on the ground a few thousand feet below."

But the lovely description of my potential death was not the only excitement.

After lunch, we learned from Julio that a team of archaeologists discovered an Incan mummy in a small ruin, not 200 yards from where we ate lunch. This team of archaeologists had been digging and excavating in this area for a few years until they found this mummy—the day we got on the trail.

A little while later, I was being led by Ryan Charlston, with Kyle Bradley right behind me. We traveled down a long slope with loose rocks and the occasional "severely pissed off" or "mildly annoyed" drop off on the right. After a while, KB took the lead and led me through a herd of cows, sheep, and goats. I heard the mooing of cattle and the bawing of sheep and goats.

Not far behind me, Anna was leading Terry, and behind Terry hiked Justin. As soon as we came in sight of cattle, Justin began wailing at the top of his voice. "Oh my God, my aching gut! Why, oh why, do you pain me so, cattle?"

Then Terry began yelling, "I see steak!"

"Let's charge them," I called back over my shoulder.

"Oh, I see steak! It's right there waiting to be taken!" Justin cried pitifully.

We were right in the heart of the herd now. And Terry and Justin started mooing back at the cows. From this point on, when Justin would guide Terry or me, the sizes of rocks would be referred to as farm animals. Relatively large rocks were half-a-cows, cows, and horses. Medium-sized rocks were hogs and pigs. Smallish rocks were chickens and chicken heads. And finally, a hodgepodge of varying-sized rocks was a "farm" or "barnyard."

We continued methodically down the trail until we came out onto the school's soccer field in Chilipahua. Our duffels formed a pile in the middle of the field with the tents set up all around them.

Dave dished out tent assignments, assigning Ryan and me as tentmates. I will never forget those two nights that I spent with Ryan as my tentmate. Not because we talked a lot or had some bonding moment—although we did have some great discussions on the best percussionists we knew. Ryan and I had played drums since the age of seven and were both very passionate about music. But I digress. I remember those two particular nights because Ryan's feet stunk to high heaven. Ryan and I stashed our bags in our tent and hurried to the meal tent to catch the end of tea-time—which was coca tea and crackers. We talked, munched on our snacks, and waited for everyone to get into camp. Eventually, when everyone was in, we had dinner. And exhausted from a long day on the trail, we went to bed.

A Day of Service

After breakfast, we found ourselves lining up on one side of a small schoolyard. On the opposite side was a line of young, small school children ranging in age from six to 11. We were there to help them paint their school. One of the Global Explorers' beliefs was community service. Wherever they traveled, the program involved a community service project. This was ours.

Each Peruvian student introduced him or herself in Spanish. And then, the two teachers welcomed and thanked us for what we were doing for their community. They explained that the Peruvian government did not give much money to education, especially to the smaller mountain communities like Chilipahua. Often, these communities are only accessible by foot.

Dave then took the floor and thanked the community of Chilipahua for welcoming us with open arms. We went around and introduced ourselves in the best Spanish we could muster. Then each group—the school children and us—performed a song that best represented our culture. We performed the "Hokie Pokie." Then it was time to paint.

Yes, a blind kid can paint the side of a schoolhouse. I do, however, stay away from trim work. I find it quite tedious.

We painted the inside and outside walls of the two-room schoolhouse blue and the doors red. And as we painted, we talked—as best we could—with the students.

What did they like to do? What was their favorite color? Did they like school? We learned that almost all the children that attended this small school often woke up at or before dawn to walk for three-plus hours over mountainous terrain to come to school. Then at the end of the school day, they would return home over that same mountainous terrain. The students were enthusiastic and eager to paint their school.

But then again, we were just as enthusiastic.

While painting an outside wall, Eric Alexander crept up behind me and painted some quick designs on my calves. As I turned to confront him about it, Alysha was letting her arm drop, and her paintbrush caught me above the left eye. We all looked a little more like Smurfs after finishing painting the school.

We washed off in the cold mountain stream that ran close by the school. After cleaning ourselves, we sat down for a traditional lunch prepared by the villagers.

The villagers built an oven by digging a pit, then placed meat and potatoes in the oven, covered them with straw and clay, and finished by collapsing the covering around the oven. The meat and potatoes slowly cooked while we painted the school. This meat and potatoes dish, cooked in this particular oven, was called Pacha Manca-meaning "Food from the Mother Earth."

We sat, ate, and talked about the morning. It was amazing how appreciative the community of Chilipahua was for our effort. When we looked at our handiwork, we saw passion and effort, but no masterpiece. But when they looked at it, they saw a fresh coat of paint and people who cared enough to help them out.

Intense games of soccer between the Supers and the Chilipahua students filled the afternoon. Terry had the idea of wrapping a plastic bag around the soccer ball so that any blind Supers who wanted to play could hear the ball moving across the ground and also participate. And while we had several talented soccer players and athletes among the Supers, we were no match for the young Peruvian students.

We finished our day of service back in the schoolyard. The community again thanked us and performed a rendition of the Peruvian National anthem. In turn, we thanked the community for welcoming and hosting us. We then sang "The Star-Spangled Banner." Then we parted. We left several gifts of books, soccer balls, and school supplies for the school.

We returned to our tents, ate dinner, and then gathered in the dining tent to listen to Jeff Evans tell us about himself and his adventures. And as Erik and Eric did before him, he related his tales in a humorous yet inspiring manner.

Jeff's Words of Wisdom

"Something I've discovered is that leaders aren't born. I was a punk as a teenager and stirred up all sorts of trouble. There was even talk of military school."

Jeff turned down a full-ride scholarship to wrestle and instead attended the University of Tennessee to party with his buddies. "I didn't have any foresight to see and know what was good for me. I had no focus and was as far away from being a leader as I could be. For me to grow up, it took surrounding myself with people with vision, to help me move forward in a positive way."

Jeff eventually found his way to Colorado and a group of people who began teaching him focus through rock climbing. "I'd done a little bit of climbing before, but not very much. So these guys invited me climbing. And when I got to the base of the rock, I didn't know how to tie a rope. They took pity on me, patted me on the head, and said, 'Grasshopper, we will teach you.'"

Climbing gave Jeff direction, which was relatable to me. Erik W had pointed me to rock climbing to give me direction when I was newly blind. And I'd find that coming back to an athletic goal or pursuit would keep me grounded in all areas of my life. And when I didn't have that focus is when I'd struggle personally and professionally.

Eventually, Jeff heard about this blind rock climber Erik Weihenmayer who wanted to start climbing big mountains. "Erik would ask people to climb with him, and everyone seemed to have a dentist appointment that day. So I figured I'd see what this guy was about."

"Erik got out of the car wearing green pants and a blue jean jacket. He looked like a bag of Skittles. It was embarrassing! So I decided we weren't going out in the mountains looking like that. What was this guy, blind or color blind?"

"Over the course of three days, I found a brother and a group of guys that I could share a collective vision with. I'd found a team."

Over several years, that team grew and became strong enough to take on Mt Everest. "Erik will be the first to tell you that he's so proud to have summitted Everest, but I'll bet you that he's more proud that we got 19 people on our team to the summit in one day. Everybody stepped up. There was never a time when somebody pointed a finger and said, "You're not pulling your weight." We worked together. When I had a weak day, there were other guys that had strong days."

As Jeff spoke, one story that stood out perfectly and demonstrated the transformational process he'd gone through from a non-leader punk kid to a teammate and full-fledged leader:

"On summit night, we reached a point where the ropes we'd been following a split and went in two different directions up to the same point. We don't need these ropes to get up, but we need them to get down just in case the weather turns bad."

"The rope to the left went through this nasty bunch of rock. The kind of terrain where you take two steps up and one step back. The kind of stuff that Erik W hates because it tears him up. And the rope to the right goes up to the same point through beautiful smoother terrain, but the rope itself is buried of two feet of frozen snow."

"So I had a choice. I could go the way where the ropes have already been dug out and risk Erik being worn out and not able to reach the summit. Or, I could dig those ropes out that go over the terrain that Erik loves at 28,000 feet, which is going to take everything I've got. I could go the easy way for me and the hard way for Erik, or the hard way for me and the easy way for Erik. So I chose to dig those ropes out, knowing that when I finished my day was done, there would be no summit for me."

"When you take yourself—as an individual—out and make it about the team and not yourself, you increase the power of your team. I was not there for me. I was not there to climb that mountain and to stand on top. I was there for Erik and to get him to the top. That was my reason for being there."

But as Jeff stood on the South Summit of Everest and watched Erik W begin making his way toward the true summit—still a two-hour journey away—he was blown away by what he was seeing. "That son of a bitch, one of my best friends, was about to stand on top of the world. And I wasn't about to hear him talk about it for the rest of his life. But more than that, I saw a blind dude doing something I could never have imagined. And so I fell in behind him, and two hours later, we stood on top of Mt Everest, along with Eric A, Didrik, and a lot of others. Nineteen of us from one team in one day."

Jeff's talk built upon Erik W's and Eric A's talks on teamwork and leadership. I was beginning to understand that we all have the capacity to be a leader. More often than not, it's in moments. We're all given opportunities to step up, and we have to have the vision and foresight to know when to step up and when to put others before ourselves. My eyes were slowly opening to the concepts of teamwork and leadership. It would take years to understand and begin putting these lessons into practice.

I recorded these talks. And for years after I came home from Peru, I would listen to them so much that I can probably recite them from memory. But more importantly, I took away the message in them. I didn't know when, I didn't know how, but I knew someday the lessons in them would be there for the taking. And I couldn't wait to learn them.

Chapter 8

Ending and Beginning

"Mmm, chokemeal!" Jeff exclaimed. It was 5:45 a.m., and we had been served a lumpy tasteless mess with fruit for flavoring. Jeff had told us early on in the trip that "food is fuel. So, make sure and eat it. Even if it tastes gross."

Then Dave announced we would be splitting up into two groups of hikers. The first group would leave at 6:30, and the second group would follow at 7. He read off names of who would be in each group, and then it was time to go. They placed me in the second group—the group of hikers that generally traveled a bit faster than those in the first group.

We set out a little after 7 o'clock. We had woken up that morning with frost on our tents, and we were all layered up. We hiked through the trees, stepping over roots, rocks, and small streams. I followed Max, who had attached my bells to a jumble of carabiners hanging from his backpack. Pretty soon, we began moving uphill, and the trees began to thin. Occasionally a child would pass us going in the opposite direction toward school.

Eventually, we came in sight of the actual village of Chilipahua. It was a cluster of thatched huts with a few goats roaming the grassy hillside. From here, we climbed to the Chilipahua Pass at 14,905 feet— our second highest point of elevation we would reach on the trip.

From the top of the pass, we gazed down a long, steep, grassy mountainside. In the distance were snowcapped peaks, and down below us was a valley with a stream.

We descended from this high point to a lunch of vegetable soup and sandwiches. On the descent, Terry slipped and strained a ligament. We had several pack horses that carried our duffle bags and an extra horse or two in case a hiker was sick or injured and could not continue to hike. Terry refused to get on a horse. "I came to hike. Not to ride a horse," he said. He pushed on and continued to be one of the strongest hikers for the remainder of the trip.

After lunch, we hiked for a little more than an hour along a relatively smooth path except for the occasional rock or stream to step over. Then we came to a steep, sandy mountainside.

The path we followed was about two feet wide and sloping off the side. Broken pieces of rock and shale covered the trail and continuously slid from our left down onto the trail and occasionally over the 200 to 300—foot drop on the right. This drop may have only been 200 or 300 feet, but there was no bouncing our way down the cliff. It overhung rapids that dashed against sharp, jagged rocks. The message was clear: don't fall, don't fall, and DON'T FALL.

When back on the trail, Terry slipped on a loose piece of shale, but Eric Alexander grabbed his backpack, keeping him upright. Even farther back, Paul—one of our less experienced blind hikers—slipped, and Jeff seized hold of him. Paul was shaken by the near fall and rode a horse the rest of the way across the ridge.

After the ridge, we cruised along reasonably easy terrain. Eric Alexander and I would occasionally kick at a rock and send it tumbling over a "mildly annoyed" drop-off on the right. Then I heard Andrew ask our assistant guide, Luis, "How much farther to camp?"

Luis replied, "Oh, no worries, my friend. It's only five minutes." "Okay, only five minutes," Andrew said.

We all walked along for about 20 minutes. Then Andrew jokingly burst out, "You dirty liar, Luis! Now tell me how much farther to camp?"

"Oh, no worries...only five minutes. I swear it's just around this next hill." As we went around the hill, Luis said, "Okay, maybe not that hill, but I'm sure it's this next one."

About an hour later, we pulled into camp after hearing Luis say, "No worries, it's over this hill. It's five minutes easy hiking." Andrew was right. Luis was "a dirty liar."

One Last Uphill Push

I woke to the sounds of Terry calling out, "Why am I half out of my tent?"

And to Didrik yelling "Carajo, apúrate!"

Max had forgotten to zip closed the bottom half of the door to the tent he shared with Terry. During the night, Terry's legs had slid downhill and out of the tent; when he woke, his lower half was out in the frosty air and his upper half in the cozy-warm tent.

We had one last push up to the highest point of our trek—Wayana Pass—at 15,020 feet. We split into groups and climbed up a steep trail. To our right was a waterfall tumbling down the cliff and a steep drop down a scree slope. We ascended 1,000 feet in less than two miles and scurried up a steep grassy slope to the top of Wayana Pass. The ascent had taken us a little under four hours.

We sat in a circle and celebrated with toasts and congratulations. "Here's to friendship."

"Here's to water."

"Here's to the highest point of the trek." "Here's to water."

"Here's to hiking downhill from here on." "One last time, let's hear it for water!"

It's All Downhill From Here

After our mini celebration, we all scattered over the hillside and picked up a rock. At the top of Wayana Pass—and many high points on trails and mountains—a pile of rocks is known as a cairn. It's tradition and respect for each person that passes the cairn to add to it. We did. Then it was time to start heading downhill.

We sped down through golden-brown fields dotted with herds of cattle and sheep. We ate lunch insight of two 200-foot-tall cascading waterfalls. Then it was just a continuous flat and downhill trek for several hours. At some points, we would need to step from rock to rock as we crossed streams about ten feet wide.

That night we built a fire and just relaxed. Jeff had a CD player and mini speakers, and we all sang along to Devil Went Down to Georgia and Ring of Fire.

Merging Trails

The following day, we bid farewell to our porters. Today would be the last day that they would carry our bags. My Dad worked for Bubba Burger, and I had brought hats and T-shirts to give to the porters. Global Explorers also presented the porters with Global Explorers T-shirts as thanks for helping us get this far.

As we hiked along the tree-covered trail, the porters and cooks lagged behind as they finished packing up the camp. Then as they led the pack horses past us, we all laughed as they were wearing their Bubba Burger hats.

We hiked along a steep gravel-strewn hillside with small narrow paths and long drop-offs. We had to be extremely careful where we put our feet. One misplaced step would send us tumbling.

By the time we arrived at lunch, we were nearly an hour behind schedule. But it cheered us up to see that the cooks and porters had all waited for us, and they all had on their Bubba Burger T-shirts and hats. They had dubbed themselves "The Bubba Burger Boys."

After a quick lunch of rice, tuna, onions, and fried potatoes—we were all getting sick of rice by now—we got back on the trail. At this point, the trail we had been following merged with the more heavily traveled standard Inca Trail. After spending nearly four days seeing only each other, and our cooks and porters, it was almost a surprise to see other travelers and tourists hiking along the gravel-strewn trail.

As we stepped onto the trail, it almost felt like there were wheels attached to our hiking boots. The trail felt almost paved, and we practically started running along the trail. We sped past people, houses, and animals. I could hear the roar of a river off to the left and far below. It was warmer and more tropical than in previous days.

Eventually, we reached the hacienda of Q'ente.

Julio had told us that we would have access to hot showers. Many people took advantage of that luxury. I, and a few others, elected not to take showers since we arrived at Machu Picchu the next day and would be able to take longer showers at our hotel. We dined on sausage, beef, and potatoes. And then watched Andrew perform a card trick. Someone would hold up a playing card, and Andrew would guess whether it was red or black. He hardly ever got one wrong. We later learned that Andrew and another Super had a secret signal that told Andrew whether the card was red or black.

After a final cup of coca tea, we went to the tents in eager anticipation of the next day.

Drink it. Don't Sniff it.

It was our equivalent of summit day. Today we would reach the ancient, sacred Inca city of Machu Picchu. After breakfast, we gathered in the center of camp. We all put our hands in the center to do a breakdown to pump ourselves up like we were a sports team. But instead of saying something motivational, popular, or sensible, like "Go team," or "Machu Picchu," on the count of three, we shouted "Coca tea!"

And then we set off toward the train station. We would take a train several miles and then get off and continue our hike up to a checkpoint.

Didrik's Words of Wisdom

As we waited for our train, our field dispatch guru and photographer, Didrik Johnck, gathered us all around to talk to us about his experiences with the outdoors, teamwork, and leadership.

"I think that leadership and being a team player really go hand-in-hand. One time, when I was in the Himalayas, we were trekking to the base of a mountain. In order to get to the base, we needed to trek over some pretty high passes—much like the passes we've gone over in the last couple of days. I was with a group of about fifteen people of all ages. We had the designated leaders—people like Dave and Julio.

"On the fourth day, we had to trek over this really high pass. It was going to be a long hard, twelve-hour day. And about halfway into the day, the clouds rolled in, and a blizzard settled right on top of us. It was pretty sketchy. Being the one with the most experience in the mountains, people immediately started looking to me as a leader. I'd been doing my thing, on the sidelines—running around taking pictures—but people were looking to me for guidance. It was one of those moments where nobody knows what to do, and everyone's waiting for someone to step up and take command.

"So I stopped the cameraman thing and grabbed some of the porters that were behind us carrying the gear. I took control of the situation.

"We set up the tents and all crammed in to keep warm. Including our porters who, quite honestly, had a different smell. But it didn't matter who you were or how bad you smelled, just get in and keep warm."

The group sat there, fifteen to twenty people in a four-person tent, waiting for the storm to pass so they could continue. Instances like this seem slight and obvious, but often, it takes someone like Didrik to guide people to the most straightforward and best course of action. In this case, stay put and stay warm to prevent a potential disaster. Didrik went on to tell us about many little moments that added up to the success of mountaineering teams he'd been on, ultimately culminating with the Everest Expedition.

"There was one particular decision we had to make as a team that sticks out in my mind," he said. The team pulled into the last camp situated at 26,000 feet up on Mt Everest. Above 26,000 feet is known as the "Death Zone," where your body can't survive for long. You can't sleep. You can't eat. So when you get up there, you don't want to stick around. You want to bang out the summit and get out; otherwise, your body is going to wither away.

Initially, the team planned to grab a couple of hours of sleep at this highest camp and immediately set out for the summit. But the last of the group rolled into camp just a few hours before they all planned to make their summit push. The entire team had had a rough day, and no one could fathom having another massive day of going for the summit and back down.

After some rest and food, the team had a decision to make. Should they do the unthinkable? Stay at 26,000 feet for a whole day and wait for the next day to go for the summit?

"In the history of Everest, people just don't stay at that altitude," Didrik told us. "All the research, everything everyone says is that you just can't stay at that altitude. And even if you do, you'll completely blow any chance you might have had at the summit. But we were totally blown out and wasted anyway. But we wondered should we buck the trend? Should we do the unthinkable and stay in the death zone an extra 24 hours?

"Our expedition leader helped facilitate that discussion, and eventually, as a team, we decided that we'd stay where we were an extra day. Everybody had input. Nobody was quiet. We went around the whole circle and asked each person, 'Should we go or should we stay?' At those times, you can't sit back and let other people make the decisions for you. And that's also part of being a team player. Everybody has an opinion. Everybody has something to say that's valuable."

"And so we stayed for a whole day. Everybody said we were crazy. The other teams that were in camp, they went on to the summit that night and successfully came back down. There was some doubt circulating through our team whether or not we'd done the right thing. It was a risky move, but we'd made that decision as a team and ultimately went on to summit and get back down successfully."

Didrik's stories reiterated that we each had the ability to recognize times where we could step up and direct traffic or contribute to the group in a small way that leads to the entire group's success.

At the time, we may not realize it, but each small action leads to another and creates a chain reaction, leading to the team's success. I wondered what small actions I could do that would lead to the success of this and future teams.

When Didrik finished speaking, we climbed on a train and rode a few miles to where the trail continued. "We have three hours to reach the next checkpoint," said Julio. "And if we don't make it in the three hours, they won't let us through."

The trail started flat with the occasional rock or root in the middle of the path. Tall trees surrounded us, and thick humid air pressed us from all sides.

Poles and Packs

Throughout the trip, the blind hikers had been guided by following the sounds of bells rung by the sighted guides and using two trekking poles to feel for the rocks, roots, and drops in the trail. Over the last couple of days, a few people found it much quicker and more accessible for the blind person to lay a hand on their sighted guide's backpack while they scanned the trail with a trekking pole. As a whole, the group was moving a little faster and sticking together more. But I was beginning to struggle.

Even though we were in the thick oxygenated air of about 7,000 feet, I was struggling to get enough air into my lungs. I would take several steps up the hill and lean heavily on my trekking poles, chest heaving. I wanted to stay at the front. I wanted to be the strongest one. But it was taking a toll.

As we began to climb up a steep series of switchbacks, Ryan led and encouraged me. Finally, after one short rest, I had to consent and grabbed onto a strap of Ryan's pack with my left hand while my right worked my trekking pole. I was constantly worried that I'd stumble and put weight on Ryan's pack and throw him off balance. But after a while, I felt semi-back to normal and was able to use both poles again.

Ah, teamwork. I was learning.

We continued winding our way up the steep jungle-covered mountainside, mosquitoes whizzed past our ears, birds twittered, monkeys screeched overhead, and the trees grew thicker and closer together.

We reached the checkpoint an hour and a half before it closed for the day, and it was there that we took our lunch break. We'd all been given a cloth lunch bag with a sandwich, crackers, and fruit. But then it was time to shoulder our packs again and set off for the last leg of our hike toward the Sun Gate.

I partnered with Kyle Bradley, and we hiked quickly but efficiently. We hiked downhill, then steeply up, and then steeply back down. K.B. would occasionally forget to mention a low-hanging branch, and I would clunk my head against it. I laughingly joked, "These branches sure are low, but at least I'm tall enough so that I hit my head on them."

Then we stepped onto a short but narrow rock-strewn ledge with a potential death fall to the right and a solid rock wall to the left. It must have just rained not long before because the rocks were slick with water. At the end of this sketchy section, K.B. and I scrambled up a sharply angled, roughly hewn stone staircase. And as we climbed over the top, we could see the Sun Gate perched atop a ridge no more than 10 minutes away.

Our group stopped and waited for twenty to thirty minutes for the rest of the team to catch up. Then we all set off together as one large team toward Machu Picchu. Ten minutes later, we were there.

I stepped across the threshold between two towering rock walls. The rock ledge beneath my feet was smooth and flat, and the whole world just seemed to open up in front of me. As Brad and I walked further out onto the ledge, allowing others to filter in behind us, I heard Justin scream to the sky, "YEEHAW!"

Terraces and Stone Steps

"Dude! It's freaking awesome!" Brad said.

Then Phil and Didrik were there standing in front of us with their cameras.

Brad described how the terraces plunged into the valley between the high mountain peaks. He described how the sun sank toward the mountaintops, flashing brilliant orange, red, and yellow colors. He took my trekking pole and pointed it toward Machu Picchu, 2,000 feet below us and surrounded by high mountains.

Then Phil and Didrik both asked me, "Kyle...how are you feeling?" "Awesome!" I said. "I'm so proud of this team for pushing through and making it here."

After handshakes, high-fives, and hugs all around, we descended the worn stone steps down many terraces into the ancient, sacred city of Machu Picchu.

Party hardy in the town with no hot watty.

We hurried through the actual city of Machu Picchu—we would have an official tour the next day—and caught the last bus leaving from the city entrance down to Aguas Calientes, where we would stay in a hotel for the night. We arrived at our hotel and immediately all wanted to take showers. However, Peruvian plumbing isn't quite up to American standards.

When everyone tried taking showers, only a small amount of water came out. And for the most part, the water was cold. When I took my shower, I had a blissful 45-second trickle of hot water, which promptly became icy. Funny, since Aguas Calientes means "hot water." After showering, we walked to dinner. However, it wasn't as much of a dinner as it was a party. Each of us ordered an individual pizza and an ice-cold bottle of Coca-Cola. I was so hungry that after polishing off my pizza, Anna and Charlotte passed their remaining slices over to me. In all, I ate the equivalent of two individual pizzas. Not a bad celebratory dinner. Dave then offered us all the opportunity to sample a Peruvian delicacy—guinea pig.

The pig was delivered and looked exactly like a guinea pig, with head and limbs still attached. The meat was a little tough and had spices cooked into it. Nobody cared to eat more than a bite or two. Erik was particularly opposed to even trying it though Jeff kept attempting to make him eat it by mistake. Jeff would drop the entire pig on Erik's plate, and Erik would shove it off. Then Jeff somehow managed to put the pig in Erik's lap. Then he held the pig by its head, and he snuck around behind Erik. He then nuzzled Erik's neck with the pig's snout. No matter what, Erik refused to eat the guinea pig.

After some laughing and talking, we Supers started talking amongst ourselves about how if not for all the adults—Erik, Eric, Jeff, Didrik, Dave, Casey, Julio—and the camera crews, we wouldn't have had such a great time. We wanted to thank them.

We elected Andrew spokesperson, and he got up from our table and went over to the table where all the adults were seated.

"We decided to get up from our salads and drinks to come over here because we know that some of you are leaving tomorrow, and we want to thank you, guys. So, without further ado, Jeff, Jefe. Throughout this trip, you've been making people drink water, and you've been there for them when they're sick. You've always been that kind of guy whom someone can turn to if they had an issue. That's always been great, so we wanted to say thank you. And we didn't get you anything."

Everyone laughed and applauded while Jeff said, "You didn't have to get me anything, bro. You gave me many memories."

"Didrik, Deeds, D Money...You've been doing all this camera stuff, and it's really cool. You know how you do the 'All right give me some love, show this camera some love!' It's been a lot of fun having you here. You're always ready to start up a conversation or ready to talk to someone. Wherever you are, there's always someone talking and always someone having fun. And I think everyone enjoyed that about you. You've helped us write our dispatches, and you've just done a great job, so thanks a lot.

"Phil and Russ, you guys, thanks for giving our story to the world. You guys came on this trip to do a job. That was your objective. It was your job to put us on film and to make money for all of us. You guys came down here with that in mind, and it's been hard to find two people that have been nicer or more friendly than you guys. Phil, I've heard from a lot of people that you are probably the nicest and purest news guy I've ever met."

There were a few chuckles, and either Phil or Russ said, "Lies all of it!"

"Russ, I was asking people what they wanted to say about you. A lot of people were saying that you're a mix between a friend and a father figure. It's so cool to have that on this trip. It was just awesome! You both are great, and I hope you guys make a lot of money off this."

"So do we, baby!" said Phil and Russ.

"And that other guy...Erik Weihenmayer. Erik, first of all, thanks for taking time out of your schedule to come down here and do this with us. But I have to tell a little story here. I sent Erik an email in January asking him if I could go on this trip. He replies to me in March, and he says, 'Hey Andrew, sorry I couldn't answer you. I was editing my book and climbing rock faces in Thailand!' And I say to myself, 'Oh, well! I'm sorry!'"

Everybody laughed heartily. Then Andrew continued, "So you're just a guy, and taking time out of your schedule to travel around the world with eighteen crazy teenage kids is really cool. You come down here, and you're supposed to be famous. You're supposed to have done all this before. Free stuff, red carpet, the whole deal. Especially for blind people, you're kind of an idol. But enough to inflate your ego. Well, I'd met you before, and I didn't exactly consult people on this but, I think a lot of people expected you to be different from who you are. In America, there's a whole stigma for celebrities. You're supposed to be super rich, super snobbish, and you're supposed to hate everyone."

Jeff cut in, "Man, he's got that figured out!"

"I don't hate on the little people," Erik said.

"You're just so cool, man! It was great to hear the stories and everything. If nobody knew it, I don't think anybody would think you're supposed to be famous. So, Erik, thank you for coming, and thank you for sharing yourself with us."

Then after a short pause, Erik said, "I'd hug you, but you're across the table."

Then Charlotte took over from Andrew to thank Bernd, Sebastian, and Mariska for their work on the documentary. "We just wanted to thank you guys for coming over here. We thought it would be odd to have a film crew here, but you guys haven't been weird. It's been great, and we've had a lot of fun getting to know you. You guys have been incredibly nice to everybody, and it's just been great. Thank you very much!"

Then Andrew stepped up again. "All right now, it's my turn again. We'd like to thank two people who made sure we didn't starve and die. That's Luis and Julio. Luis, como estas amigo? I don't know where to begin in thanking you, Luis. I also have no idea where you came from. One day Julio just kind of said, 'Here's Luis.' and then you were like, 'Hey ma friend, how's it going?' At the beginning of the trip, we celebrated your birthday. But the one thing that people must know about Luis is that he is a dirty liar. And for those of you who aren't laughing, I'll tell the story. On the trail, Luis would stop, and we would ask, 'How much further? I can't breathe. I can't walk. I need help; my knee's busted I'm in amazing pain.' And Luis would say, 'Oh, five minutes, no worries!' Twenty minutes later, 'Luis, I'm dying here!'

"No, no, it's okay. Five minutes, just over this hill. Okay, maybe not that hill but the next one.' But Luis, we celebrated your birthday, we suffered with you, we went through a lot of things with you, and you're just great. So, thank you so much.

"Our next thank you goes to a very especial person." Everyone cracked up. "JULIO! You were another person that just showed up. We were just introduced to you, 'Here's Julio, ' and then you say, 'Here's Saqsayhuman.' You got us through this trip. You knew everything about all the places we visited. You're a great tour guide, and you do your job very well. So, thank you very much."

Then Ryan thanked Eric Alexander. "Eric, you're wicked awesome, and everyone knows that. You go around just like everyone's your friend, and you don't care what others think about you. I think that's a special quality that not a lot of people have. Even when you were placed over at the kid's table, you didn't care, and I just thought that was awesome. It's not enough, but we just want to say thank you for everything you've done for us."

Then Andrew said, in a very mellow tone, "We'd also like to thank two people that without them, this trip would not be possible. And that would be Hector and Flaveo!" Everyone laughed. "No, no, it's

Casey and Dave," Andrew said. "Casey, I'm trying to think of things to say about you because everyone told me, 'Andrew, we have too much to say about Casey, so just make it up.' So, all I can say, Casey is, without you on this trip, it wouldn't have been the same."

Then Dave stood up and said, "Okay, now that that's over with!" Everyone shouted him down.

"Sit down, Dave. You're not getting away with it so easily." Everyone was laughing, and then Andrew said our thanks to Dave.

"Dave Shurna. The first time I came in contact with Dave, Erik had sent me this email saying, 'Dave Shurna wants to know if you want to go on this trip.' So, I sent Dave this email saying, 'Hi Dave Shurna, I'm Andrew Johnson, and I would feel appreciative, and it would warm my heart if you would let me go on this trip.' I made it fluffy, and with every key that I typed, I was thinking, 'Please let me go!' But on this trip, we found out that Dave Shurna is not the president of the United States. You can actually have a conversation with him. The thing is, I think there are two Dave Shurnas. There's the Dave Shurna that stands in front of everybody talking about important things like sickness, and statistics, and being a good leader. And then there's just Dave who stands up there speaking rapid-fire Spanish and is always urging everyone to have a good time when he's just like one of the kids up there having a good time himself. I have no doubt that this trip could not have happened without both Dave Shurnas. Dave, you're pretty cool.

"We just want to thank all of you guys. Something someone said to me when I turned 13 was that adults always keep their eyes on us. We're always the group under suspicion, and we're being watched. On TV shows, it's always us that get vilified and portrayed badly. But all of you haven't treated us like that. You haven't treated us like kids. You've treated us as equals. You didn't look down on us, and you weren't condescending. You didn't try to overrule us with your superiority, and that means a lot to all of us. Thank you so much. You guys are amazing."

We all gave an enthusiastic round of applause. And then Jeff hopped up and announced that the adults had a special little gift for us.

Jeff began, "You've all seen Letterman, right? Well, we've taken his Top 10, and we've made the 11 ways you know you're an Inca. And without further ado..."

The 11 Ways You Know You're An Inca:

(A collection of inside jokes from the Leading The Way 2006 expedition.)

11. You know you're an Inca when you go to your local 7-11 and ask for "Coca tea, hot watta."

10. You know you're an Inca when you are up in your room at home and yell down to your mother, "Bring me my sandwich, carajo, apúrate."

9. You know you're an Inca when you come to a town called Agua Caliente, and you can't find one drop of hot water in the whole place.

8. You know you're an Inca when you can entertain yourself for six hours with "Blue moon!"

(This was a riddle game we played for hours to entertain ourselves on the trails.)

7. You know you're an Inca when you walk downtown in your local community and say to everyone you pass, "This is a very especial park bench."

6. You know you're an Inca when you'd much rather play with a soccer ball covered in cow crap or a plastic bag rather than a brand new one.

5. You know you're an Inca when you can't picture a stone under your feet, but you can see the color of a playing card 20 feet away.

4. You know you're an Inca when you dream of the Inca Emperor, but he looks like Dave Shurna, and he's ringing a bell.

3. You know you're an Inca when your parents tell you, "You're fat, lazy, you watch too much TV," and your response is, "Now let me make sure I understand you."

2. You know you're an Inca when your teacher calls for quiet, and you stand up in the back row and say, "Currok!"

1. You know you're an Inca when you can very clearly distinguish the elusive creature known as uphomie.

Promises, Plans, and Preparation

After all this, the evening seemed to fly. We all promised each other that we would keep in touch and hoped this wouldn't be our last trip together. Little did we know what would be around the next corner.

The next day we toured Machu Picchu.

Officially discovered in 1911 by the American explorer Hiram Bingham, Machu Picchu sits high in the Peruvian Andes. It's known as the Sacred City of the Incas. When Bingham discovered the city, being led by a Quechua Indian boy, he looked down on a city overgrown with jungle vegetation. Bingham and his explorer crew attempted to clear out the vegetation and take many artifacts home to the United States. However, Bingham and his crew accidentally destroyed many parts of Machu Picchu, not having proper archaeological training or tools to do the job correctly.

Since its discovery in 1911, archaeologists have been slowly excavating jewels, pottery, temples, and mummies, from the ruins. We learned all of this while we walked up and down steep stone steps between high rock walls and went in and out of sacred temples and dwellings.

We were allowed to touch the famous Sacred Sundial. Terry laid down on the Sacrificial Stone and pretended he was a sacrifice to the Inca gods.

We entered one open-air temple. Around the walls of the temple were little alcoves where the Incas would put gold and silver idols. However, Julio encouraged us to stick our heads into the alcoves, and then on his command, all hum. We split into two groups, and one group did the humming while the other group listened. Then we switched.

When it was my turn to listen, I stood in the center of the temple and heard as the humming sounds echoed and reverberated around and through me. Way cool!

Then it was time to go. But as we were leaving, our group came in contact with an American family that had a young boy who was blind. (Talk about randomness.) The even cooler part of it was that they knew exactly who we were. The mom had printed out all our bios from the Global Explorers website. We all shook the little boy's hand, took some pictures, and heard about his family's trip. Then we proceeded down to Aguas Calientes.

Later that afternoon, we caught the train heading from Machu Picchu to Cusco. We had three hours to kill. And for several of us, those three hours were spent dreaming and scheming.

I overheard Justin and Terry in the row behind me talking about how it would be cool to continue climbing together as a team. How we were all inspired by what we had done and wanted to keep on doing it. And as I sat, munching on some cookies and sipping an Inca cola, I began to wonder what would be the actual next step up from Peru.

Maybe something a little bigger, a little steeper, and maybe a little more challenging. Then it hit me.

I whirled around, propped myself up on my knees, leaned over the back of my seat, and said, "Guys! What about Kilimanjaro?"

Chapter 9

The Right Moves

As great as Peru was, it did not come simply by climbing. Many other influences impacted my trek up the mountain. One of the most significant contributors to the discipline necessary for mountain climbing was the lessons learned while wrestling. And it is important to take a break from climbing to tell you the full wrestling story.

My family lived in four different houses when I was growing up. As our family grew, we needed more space. My parents' good friend was a realtor, and he kept finding "great deals." When I was three years old, my family lived in Orange Park, Florida, a large residential community outside Jacksonville.

Just to put one stereotype to rest: Yes, you can rearrange furniture and not drive blind people crazy—sometimes. You even put them in a different house, and they get around just fine.

This particular house, though, is the one in my earliest memories. What I remember most about it during the four years we lived there was the carpet. It was an oatmeal beige Berber carpet. At least, that's what my mom explained to me years later, since I wasn't a child prodigy flooring expert. Berber carpet, trendy when I was three, was made with tightly woven large loops, and homeowners liked it because it didn't show footprints or wear. With three young children in the house, my mom vacuumed all the time—because she had to. We were busy little kids, and we spent a great deal of time on the floor, playing with blocks, Legos, watching TV, and all the stuff little kids do. Mom wanted to keep the house clean.

But for me, that carpet is embedded in my memory. When people invite me to their home and describe the decor to me, if they say, "and our floors are carpeted," I picture that oatmeal-colored Berber carpet from our Orange Park house. That's because I spent lots of time with my face planted on it. I attribute that to my Dad.

My Dad loved to wrestle. He would come home from work, and after he got his work clothes off, while we were waiting for dinner, he'd grab me, pick me up off the floor, drop to his knees, and we became a tangle of legs and arms and screams and cries. Sometimes I think he only had the advantage because I laughed so hard, and I couldn't wrestle him back. Well, that and the fact that he outweighed me by more than 150 pounds.

When he was in high school, my Dad's physical education teacher was the school's wrestling coach. He added lots of wrestling to the curriculum. My Dad and his classmates would roll out the team's wrestling mats, and the coach taught them basic moves. The school team was pretty good, and several guys on the team went on to win multiple Illinois state championships.

When I was three, my Dad began to teach those basic moves to me. Of course, it was all coated in good fun. It wasn't a lesson as much as it was time to goof around, burn off some of my boundless energy, and create great memories with my Dad. But make no mistake, some serious moves were going on. Even as a little kid, I could do a respectable cradle and a decent half nelson.

When I lost my first eye, the wrestling didn't stop. It didn't stop when I lost my second eye, either. Like all of us, my Dad wanted life to continue as normal as possible, so he made sure the serious moves on the carpet I could no longer see continued, and it built in intensity.

Meeting Erik Weihenmayer right after I went blind cemented my interest in wrestling. He was on his high school team and placed second in the state championship.

The good news was that I was getting bigger, and heavier, and stronger, and my Dad's advantage dwindled with every inch and pound I put on. Losing my sight did not take away my competitive spirit or my love of sports. Wrestling was a way to fuel both, and it would play a huge role in my development as a person.

Somewhere in the Middle

I started middle school in Fall 2003. My parents wanted a school that would challenge me academically and, secondarily, offer me opportunities for sports. They began making appointments at different public and private middle schools and arranging tours. I was blind for five years by this point, but it hadn't slowed me down in spirit. My older sister, Cassandra, was also a huge motivator for me. She was brilliant and athletic, earning top grades and notoriety as a soccer player. There was no way I would let anything—even blindness—prevent me from being as good a student and athlete as my sister.

Like I have said, I was a very, very competitive person from the day I was born. Now, as an adult, I can admit I am grateful to Cassandra for being extremely talented. If I had a mediocre older sister, I probably wouldn't have achieved half of what I did in my youth.

My parents checked out four schools. We hoped to find a school with a wrestling team that would welcome me.

The two private schools were Bolles Academy, known for developing Olympic swimmers, and Episcopal High School, which had sixth through twelfth grade and a wrestling team. The two public schools were James Weldon Johnson and Darnell Cookman. We visited the schools, talked to them about how they would handle my blindness, and most important to me, what kind of sports would be available for me.

Overall, I have to say any fear or apprehension of middle school I might have had went away after talking to the administrators and teachers at these schools. Everyone we met was nice and encouraging. In the end, it came down to James Weldon Johnson and Episcopal. The deciding factor was how open-minded the teachers at James Weldon Johnson were. Talking to them, I became very excited, even though going there meant being on a wrestling team would have to wait three more years.

But I never stopped thinking about it. I certainly didn't stop wrestling with my Dad, even though I was becoming serious competition for him. He was getting up slower the older I got.

Advanced Course

Before I knew it, it was time to go to high school.

My first choice was Paxson School for Advanced Studies. This renowned preparatory high school ranked nationally and is known for high academic standards. Their esteem made it my first choice. As if the reputation and standards were not enough, Cassandra also went there. And she was doing well, igniting a fire to not only do as well but better than her.

In Spring 2006, at the end of my eighth-grade year, my parents and I met with Paxson's vice principal, Dr. Kelly Coakerdaniel. She mapped out the classes I would take, and she talked to me about Paxson and its philosophy. Then, she asked me what activities I liked. I told her about rock climbing. I knew schools didn't have rock climbing teams, so I asked, "Do you have a wrestling team?"

She said they did, and she encouraged me to try out and meet with the coach. This excited me more than I can tell you.

There was no guarantee I would get into Paxson since you have to meet admission requirements and academic standards. Plus, they had never had a blind student before. Nevertheless, I did get in, and I started ninth grade in August 2006. I had a vision teacher there, Susan Kahn. As fate would have it, Mrs. Kahn shared an office with the coordinator of the International Baccalaureate program, Mary Brightenbach. One of the IB students, Cameron Suarez, was captain of the wrestling team. He was a senior, and Mrs. Kahn and Mrs. Brightenbach arranged for us to have lunch together one day in October.

Cameron was great. Over lunch, he learned of my carpet wrestling with my Dad and how competitive I was. He encouraged me, saying things like, "We would love to have you on the team." At the end of our lunch, he said, "Come to the TANK," which is the room's name where the team practiced. Then he added, "Our first meeting is next Tuesday. We'll practice, and then tryouts are two weeks later."

The following Tuesday, I tapped my way with my cane to the TANK, my heart pounding and my palms sweaty. Cameron met me near the door and introduced me to Coach Israel Fuller. I knew about Coach Fuller. He had been an assistant football coach at Paxson, and he had wrestled when he was in high school, making it to state. He was an excellent, hard-nosed wrestler. His value as a coach was that he knew the Florida wrestling circuit, and he knew what it took to get guys there.

I listened to everything he told me each afternoon at those practice sessions in the TANK. I would come home and show my Dad what I had learned. While Dad had taught me the basics, I didn't know double leg or single leg or takedowns or specific techniques. My Dad became a willing partner as I worked on the moves, putting everything I had into them. I like to think there were a few times my Dad was very grateful when mom called us to dinner.

At tryouts, I worked very hard every afternoon. I was intensely focused. I made the team with no problem because we sucked.

Paxson is known for academics, not athletics. The last state championship the school won was in basketball in 1965. I was not on the team to rack up ribbons and trophies, which was good because I would have been very disappointed. Instead, wrestling taught me many lessons that I would remember long after my last match was over.

A Body in Motion

Wrestling is a challenging, gritty, gritty sport. Being a wrestler makes you a harder person. Since I lost my vision and had the typical teenage angst, this hardness was what I needed to grow up, process my loss, and prepare myself for living my life.

Matches are won in practice. You can say that about any sport, and I certainly learned that with wrestling. Practice is where you learn the essential fundamentals, and you master them. Every day, Coach Fuller ran practice and encouraged peer teaching. The seniors were the ones who taught me technique, the proper technique. Cameron would tell me, "If you never see the bad technique, then you won't develop bad technique yourself." He repeated this phrase my freshman year, and it sunk in.

I have told myself that learning things the right way from the start as I have faced new situations in my life—the basics matter. Get the details down. It has paid off for me every time.

Coach Fuller and Cameron also picked up where my Dad left off. They taught me how to move in the ring and not just scrapple on the mat. It was little stuff, fundamentals. However, it made all the difference in the world. They taught me that when you are on your feet, stay on the balls of your feet. Do not rock back onto your heels because it gives you better balance and can move quicker.

They also taught me the importance of staying low, which means you have to bring your hips down and your knees are at a 90-degree angle the entire match. It takes tremendous athleticism and strength to accomplish the right angle, especially in your thigh muscles, which is why the elite wrestlers are in such great shape.

I think wrestling appealed to me because it was such a good fit for my personality. I have heard coaches describe wrestling as a series of anaerobic and aerobic exercises. As a wrestler, in the ring, you are constantly moving, constantly in motion. And then, at the precise right time, you have to have bursts of energy. If you asked my Mom, I think she would say this described me as a toddler, an adolescent, and a teenager perfectly. I never sat still. I moved very quickly. Blindness did nothing to change that about me. Wrestling gave me a place to use it.

For the Record

The wrestling rule book has accommodations for blind wrestlers. My opponents and I started with a palm motion in the middle of the ring —one palm up and one palm down. The ref blows the whistle, and we can move, as opposed to two sighted wrestlers who just look at each other and then lunge for appendages when the whistle blows. During the match, the sighted wrestler cannot break contact with me at any time. He has to keep a hand, a knee, a foot in contact with my body at all times. That's how I know where he is. I had to learn to read an upside-down kneecap, a sideways elbow, so I could figure out—in a split second—where the other parts of his body were. Because of this constant contact, a blind wrestler can have a strong advantage—especially when on the ground.

I wish I could tell you that advantage turned me into a champion in my rookie season. But my record was pitiful. The only reason I won my first match was that my opponent's shoulder hit me below my left eye. I felt my left eye falling and managed to push my opponent away, reach up and catch the eye, crying out, "Oh shit! My eye!"

I stepped away from my opponent as he looked up and saw my open socket. My teammates would later tell me that he jumped about a foot and a half in the air and about four feet back. I calmly popped my eye back in the socket, and the referee brought us back to the center of the mat. Within 30 seconds, I had a takedown and a pin—ending the match.

I took the victory.

The winning was great. I did win matches. And by my junior year, I was winning more matches than I lost. During my senior year alone, I won more matches than my first three years combined. All the fundamentals and the commitment at practice started paying off.

Additionally, my parents found great camps for me to attend. I spent two summers at a wrestling camp and learned from Olympic wrestler Ken Chertow. Ken used me to demonstrate moves and techniques, and this helped me a ton. Since I couldn't see the position of his arms, hands, and knees, by placing me on the mat and explaining to the other campers what the positions and moves meant strategically, I could feel it. Thus, I could use it later on.

During the Christmas break of my senior year, my parents gave me a great present. They sent me to Ken's training camp in Philadelphia. I left the day after Christmas and came home on New Year's Eve. It was six solid days of busting my butt. And I loved it.

Now, if you'd ever seen a wrestling camp, you would be surprised I told you I loved it. Wrestling camp is not fun. It's grueling. You are wrestling for six or seven hours a day, wrestling guys who are way better than you and getting slammed to the mat over and over. A coach from North Carolina nearly broke my arm, demonstrating technique with me.

However, the harder it got, the harder I worked. I think wrestling ingrained in me a strong work ethic, fueled by my need to push myself physically and mentally. It paid off, too. My senior year was my best season. With two weeks left in the season, my record was 21-3. My overall high school record would be 45-33, considered pitiful since you have to have 100 wins—or one or more State Titles—to get any kudos. But, if you compare this to my senior year, I made over half my wins in that one year.

Each season, we had the conference championship, and your record determines your seed for the tournament. Because my senior season was so good, I found myself slated for the number one seed for my weight class at the conference.

As an aside, for just about my entire high school wrestling career, I was in the 171-pound weight class. I had spent my freshman year wrestling at 160 pounds and then my final three years at 171. The classes from 160 to 185 are the toughest, as there is the highest number of guys in that weight class. The wrestlers who make the team for that slot are usually the best wrestlers on the team. It's just a numbers thing. And the luck of your genetic makeup if you are naturally lighter or heavier for your age.

Two weeks before the end of my regular senior season, we went to a tournament at Terry Parker High School.

I had lost my second match to my rival Jayln Lee. It was heavily anticipated match, and I was mad about the loss. I took that anger of losing out on my next opponent, and I was winning well. Late in the match, he had my ankle between his legs, and I tried to pull it out, and he wrenched the other way. I heard a "pop," and I knew it was hurt. I wrestled through it on one foot. I hung on and won 12 to 8.

However, it ended my state-run. We were two weeks away from districts. I wanted to be in the finals badly. Our school grew from my junior year to my senior year, and we went from 1A to 2A. If we had stayed 1A, I had a shot at placing at the state tournament.

As hard as it was, it taught me to persevere. I went to physical therapy and worked hard at it. I saw the payoff. I was able to compete at districts and placed fourth. On a good ankle, I probably would have placed third. But I was thrilled just to be able to compete and place at all.

Looking back on high school, I would tell you that I didn't like it very much. Academically it was hard. It was a ton of work due to two things. First was the high academic standards and rigor at Paxson. On top of that, I had to work harder as a blind student, especially in math. My fierce competitiveness would not let me coast with Cs. I was not going to give up, whining that it was just too hard. I was going to get grades as good as—if not better—than Cassandra's. I was also going to be an athlete.

With athletics added to my schedule, I would leave the house at 7 in the morning and not get home until eight at night. Then I had to eat dinner and do homework, most nights until midnight. And then it started all over again the next day. I had meets on Tuesday and Wednesday nights and tournaments on weekends. Every weekend.

It was a pace that made me weary after four years, and there was a part of me that just wanted it to be over.

However, I did love wrestling. It was not just the competition and the physical challenge and the satisfaction I got out of improving and winning. It was the tight bond I had with the guys on the team. All my friends in high school had connections to wrestling in one way or another. We hung out. We ate lunch together. We had tons of fun on the bus to and from matches. These were the guys who gave me their elbow so I could run alongside them. I wanted this time to go on forever. As I saw high school ending in my junior year, I was ready to leave but not ready to give up what I had gained on the wrestling team. So, I began to send emails to college coaches.

A College Course

Jason Balma was the coach of the club wrestling team at the University of Central Florida in Orlando, which is about three hours from my home in Jacksonville. As a club team, UCF wrestling operates under the Sports Club Council. Coach Balma had graduated from UCF and wrestled for them and became the coach immediately after graduating.

While the NCAA doesn't sanction it, it's still a very serious operation. UCF has won three national championships in wrestling.

I learned all this on UCF's website and from Google searches as I checked out colleges. My top choices were the University of Florida, Gainesville (the Gators), and UCF (the Knights).

I started emailing Coach Balma my junior year. I sent him my stats, and I asked if I could walk on and join the team. To my delight, he responded to me, and we began to correspond. He told me that if I ever wanted to come to campus, he would arrange for me to meet some of the wrestlers, and they would show me around.

He was so welcoming, like everyone I talked to at UCF—the admissions staff, the folks in Student Disability Services (who ensure accommodations for me in classes, like test-taking). UCF immediately became high on my list, and I was accepted. However, I was waiting to hear from the University of Florida, and since many members of my family are Gator fans, I had not made up my mind.

It came time for my senior regional tournament. I found out a few days before I would be wrestling a guy from Gainesville High School. The night before the tournament, in a move to psych myself up, I told my parents, "If I win, I am going to the University of Florida. If I lose, I am not."

In the first thirty seconds of the match, it was close. My opponent received some good calls. Right before the end of the first period, I got a bad call. He pinned me. I called my Mom, and she had checked the University of Florida's website and found out I didn't get in.

To be honest, I was relieved because I was leaning toward UCF.

I emailed Coach Balma, and he set up a meeting with wrestlers at UCF. We arranged a weekend for me to visit, and my parents drove me to UCF's sprawling campus. That is when I met Alex Chiricosta, or "Cherry," a freshman on the team. UCF was in the midst of its best season in five years and had just returned from the Conference Championship where the Knights dominated. Then UCF won nationals.

I kept up with this from home, and I thought it was pretty cool. "They want me on their team," I said to myself. "Wow. I get to wrestle for a winning team." That was a first.

The Underhook Thing

I entered college in the summer term at UCF, and I worked out with the team in the afternoons. Coach introduced me to Nick Christian, who had transferred from a Division 3 school. He wound up being captain my sophomore year.

Two days a week during the summer, we are holding a pretty intense practice, and I realize very quickly that wrestling on the college level is very different from high school.

Basically, my new teammates used me as a mop for the mat.

I got a little discouraged. But I was learning much more at the college level, more than I ever had in high school. Coach Balma and the captains would specialize the techniques for each wrestler—including me. Every wrestler has different strengths and styles. The goal is to make your weaknesses stronger, and your strengths darn near impossible for your opponent to handle. For example, my weakest area of wrestling was when we were on our feet needing a takedown. Coach Balma and the captains would watch me wrestle. Then they would notice little details that, if we could fix, would allow me to get better angles and put me in better positions to take a shot and get a takedown. "Try this," they would say. "We need to adjust your stance. Bring your feet wider and lower your hips. Plant your forehead right in the sucker's temple or in the cradle between his ear and neck. Feel how his shoulder is positioned. Yank on his wrist or elbow and make him step into that death grip you've got."

In high school, my strength as a wrestler was that I was a good leg rider. This meant that when we were on the ground, and I was in control—the offensive wrestler—I would slide one or both of my legs through and around my opponent's legs. The rider technique allowed me to hold and control my opponent much easier. In college, I only

got better. Coach Balma showed me how to make small adjustments, especially regarding
my hips and where they should and shouldn't be when I was in my leg riding position. The coaches also got me training on my upper body—lifting weights and increasing my strength.

Gripping Lessons

I will never forget Coach Balma telling me and the others: When the whistle blows, you lock onto your opponent and never let go.

His words were not some grand epiphany. Ken Chertow had been trying to pound that same message into my head for two years of summer and winter break camps. In college, though, it finally sank in.

One way Coach Balma tried to teach us never to let go was a technique called "hand fighting." I had heard the term in high school, and it usually referred to simply getting control of your opponent's wrists and hands. However, UCF had a different definition.

"Hand fighting" didn't just work on holding onto the opponent; it also was a way to develop aggression and an offensive mindset. A round of hand fighting might go like this: I face off with my drill partner—usually Daniel Polaski, Philip Teveras, or William Lipplet—and when the whistle blew, we latched on and climbed up our partner's arms, trying to gain control of their elbows and shoulders. We would smash our foreheads into each other's temples or necks. Sometimes we'd get a hand or two around the back of our partner's neck and yank him from side to side or straight down toward the mat. All the while, our feet are moving, circling, always propelling our bodies forward—all with EXTREMELY HIGH INTENSITY. I would often walk away from a hand fighting session with multi-colored bruises going from my eyes down the side of my face and along my neck to my shoulder.

Today, when I face a new challenge, Coach Balma's words ring in my ears: Lock on and never let go, and always attack. To me, that means never giving up and to keep on fighting no matter what.

In no way was this lesson more evident than my most defining match in college.

In November of my freshman year, I was wrestling in the UCF Open—a tournament that UCF hosted each year and invited some big-time schools to come and wrestle in. It was my last match of the tournament, and slated to wrestle Rodrigo Calergos from Florida State University. A teammate told me, "You should kick this guy's butt. All he does is a low single, and if you stop him from doing that, then you'll have no problem." I went into the match positive I was going to win. However, Calergos was quicker and stronger than I anticipated. The funny thing was I knew exactly what he was going to do, and I forgot to "hold on and be aggressive." I lost the match in 58 seconds. I was embarrassed and vowed to work harder, so I would win if I faced FSU again.

I did get the opportunity for a rematch with Calergos in February at the Seminole/Rattler Invitational—the tournament that FSU and Florida A & M University co-hosted (ironic, right?). Calergos and I were in the "Consolation Semi-Finals," meaning that our match-winner would then wrestle for third place in the tournament. This was my first legitimate opportunity to place in a college tournament, and I remembered my embarrassing loss to Calergos back in November. This time, I didn't forget to hold on and attack. With less than 30 seconds to go in the match, we were tied 5-5. In college wrestling, one of the ways you can earn an extra point is to win the "riding time." Riding time refers to the amount of time you spend on top and in control of your opponent. This is where my leg riding benefitted me greatly. To receive the one point awarded for riding time, you need to be in control of your opponent for a total of two minutes more than he is in control of you.

With the clock winding down toward 0:00, my friend and teammate Nick Christian—who was coaching me along with our assistant Coach Johnny Rouse—was screaming at me, "hold on, hold on! If you hold on, you'll get riding time!" I heard the voices of Ken Chertow and Jason Balma in my head, "Hold on and attack." I held on! Calergos collapsed beneath me as the ref blew his whistle, yelling "Time!" I won the match 6-5. I went on to take fourth place in the 174-pound weight class. I had not given up. I had worked hard to strengthen my weaknesses and improve on my strengths.

Game Changer

In my first year of college, my wrestling career went from face plants on my family's carpet to face plants on the sweaty college mats. However, the reward was all this new physical and mental training I was getting. The result? Every college match that I wrestled well on my feet, I wound up winning. This is due to my under hook series.

I would drive my left arm underneath my opponent's armpit and then wrap/hook it over the top of his shoulder. From this position, I had a very tight hold and greater control of my opponent. It allowed me to set the match's pace and kept my opponent closer to me, thereby limiting his movement and allowing me better access and ability to feel his body position and where his feet and legs were.

The combination of my leg riding, which I executed well in high school, and the underhook became my strongest technique in college. The combination communicated to me the location of my opponent and every move he made. It taught me to see his moves without my eyes.

I have the upperclassman to thank for that, and Coach Balma.

The summer after my freshman year wrestling for UCF, I worked at an outdoor camp called Sanborn. It changed my view of life and was the kickstart to a new chapter in my life.

When I returned for my sophomore year, the make-up of the wrestling team had changed. The upperclassman who had mentored me through my first year, and became my good friends, were gone. The rest of the team were great guys, but it was different. Wrestling felt different because I was different.

I stopped wrestling halfway through my sophomore year. What I learned as a wrestler has kept going. Coach Balma shared a great quote from the famous wrestler Dan Gable: "The first period is won by the wrestler with the best technique. The second period is won by the one in the best shape. The third period is won by the wrestler with the biggest heart."

I couldn't agree more. Or, as we all say after a bad match, "It's not how you fall. It's how you get up.

Even though I stopped wrestling, those quotes still defined my life. I was experiencing different things, like that summer at Sanborn. I learned new opportunities, like becoming a spinning instructor and working at the UCF Recreation and Wellness Center. Mostly, I heard a different call.

As you'll see, I followed the call, and I walked out of the ring a winner.

Chapter 10

Big Mountain

Stretching out luxuriously on a full-length mattress in a hut at 12,340 feet up a mountainside wasn't a bad way to end the day. Then Eric walked in and said, "Hey guys, we have a problem. We only have six beds in here, and there are seven guys. Someone's going to have to go over to the other side and bunk with the girls."

Max immediately volunteered. "Okay! I'll take one for the team." "Yeah, sorry, Max. But it's going to have to be one of the blind guys."

"Well, I'm half-blind. Does that count?" asked Justin. "Sorry, but you're out too."

Growing up with a Mom and three sisters, it would not have been terrible to bite the bullet and go bunk with the girls. However, I was already too settled in and comfortable. And then Terry walked in and asked, "Hey guys, where's my bed."

Pause...

"Uh, Terry, you have to sleep with the girls."

It was our fifth full day in Tanzania, almost exactly a year from when we'd been in Peru together. It was like we had never separated. The good-natured kidding and joking had continued through email, conference calls, through the airports in Detroit and Amsterdam, and now up on Kilimanjaro itself.

Plan Review

The previous year's trip had ignited a fire in many of us "Supers," participants of the Global Explorers trips, and we craved more adventure. But more than that, we craved to have more adventure together. We had bonded and become so close in Peru that we all considered each other family. Justin, Terry, and I had spearheaded this year's trip to Kilimanjaro.

On the train heading from Machu Picchu to Cusco, we'd spread out through the train and talked to certain Supers that we felt might be interested in pushing the envelope a little further and making another trip. We asked Eric Alexander if he would lead us on Kili. And as our planning commenced, Dave Shurna sent out a mass email to those of us who were planning to take on Kilimanjaro. He asked whether Global Explorers could organize our trip again. We gladly accepted and thus began a second Leading the Way Expedition.

We went through the same conference calls process and studied up on Tanzanian culture, blindness, and the Kilimanjaro environment. And in June 2007, we found ourselves meeting up in Detroit to fly to Tanzania.

Eric, Terry, and I were the first to arrive in Detroit, with everyone else close behind. Terry and I were playing cards when Jill and Charlotte arrived. Then the four of us headed toward Justin's gate to meet him. By accident, we were standing on a moving walkway going toward Justin's gate, and Justin was standing on a moving walkway heading toward us. As we passed each other, Jill called to Justin to meet us at the end of the walkway. Justin turned around—on the walkway—and began walking.

"Why aren't I going anywhere?" he called out to us as we doubled over, laughing hysterically. Eventually, he made it onto the right moving walkway, and we all continued to Alysha's gate. By the time we all arrived back to the main group, Brad, Max, Ryan, and Casey had arrived. Anna was the only one missing due to her canceled flight. She would be joining us in the next couple of days in Africa.

We had just enough time to grab a bite to eat at McDonald's, and then it was onto the plane bound for Amsterdam.

You typically hear people complain about how long transcontinental flights are, how it sucks that you can't lay back and get a good sleep. Or, by the end, you are too irritable and cranky to doing anything once you arrive at your destination. That wasn't exactly the case with our group.

Charlotte and I were sitting behind Brad and Justin. Each seat had a TV for us to watch movies. But Justin had loaded some "Blue Collar" comedy on his iPod and had brought a headphone splitter. I plugged into his iPod and spent the first two to three hours choking back hysterical laughter.

After a couple of more hours and movies, Justin gave me a dramatic description of the sunrise. "As we fly through the blue abyss, we can see out our port side window the glorious fiery ball in the cosmos that we call the sun. It hovers just above the peaks of puffy white snowcapped clouds. We can now see the future ahead."

Then the wheels went down, seats back in place, and tray tables up for touchdown in Amsterdam. Brad and I went searching for food and wound up paying the extravagant price of 12 US dollars for a total of six small pancakes, two tiny cartons of orange juice, and no syrup at...wait for it...McDonald's.

Then it was back on a plane bound for Kilimanjaro International Airport, Arusha, Tanzania, Africa.

Tanzania Arrival

As the stage lights faded and a gentle mist started to fall over the screaming crowd, a soft electric guitar played. At each pick of the string, gentle colors seemed to float out from the stage to the audience. Suddenly, a smell of soap filled my nose, and I felt a gentle brushing across my cheek. Something wrong with this picture? The screaming crowd faded along with the colors and fog, but the smell of soap increased. And the gentle brushing on my cheek suddenly became Justin slapping me in the face with a moist towelette saying, "Wakey, wakey, K Coon!"

"What the hell!" Laughter. "You SOB!" I exclaimed as I snatched the moist towelette from his hand.

I'd fallen asleep during the eight-hour flight from Amsterdam to Tanzania. During the flight, the flight attendant came by and gave everyone a moist towelette after their meal. Justin decided to have a bit more fun with his and used it to wake me up.

This little episode became a long-standing joke between Justin and me. I was trying to keep a journal and had written this account down on my computer. I then made the JAWS program, the software blind people use to transcribe written text into speech, read what I had typed. JAWS pronounces each word and inflects what it thinks should be correct. It also says "quote" whenever there's something in quotations. Justin would constantly say, "Quote, what the hell! Quote, you SOB," whenever the fancy took him.

Eventually, we started to descend, and then, after a long time, we landed.

"Jambo!" "Mambo." "Poa." "Asante sana!" Swahili phrases came at us from all sides.

Walking out of the airport, we heard a Tanzanian choir singing. Ryan described the trees, "The trunks are skinny, and the branches start very high up. It almost looks like a giant mushroom."

We loaded onto a bus and drove to our hotel. And, exhausted after a long day of travel, we fell asleep.

Meeting the Students

"Who enjoyed sleeping in their pretty princess beds?" Eric asked over a breakfast of scrambled eggs, toast, fruit, and a hot dog-like sausage that Terry christened "tube steak." Each bed had a bundle of pink mosquito netting that you could untie and hang around the bed to keep out the malaria-carrying mosquitos. We were all on anti-malaria pills, but you could never be too careful.

When Justin walked into the room he and Terry were sharing; he wondered what the bundle of pink netting above the bed was. When he found out the use, he asked, "Well, are we supposed to untie this and let it hang down?"

And Eric said, "Only if you want to look like a pretty, fairytale princess."

Once we finished breakfast, the team drove to meet up with a group of Tanzanian students. This particular group of students consisted of 10 blind and 10 sighted. Together we'd all learn about each other: blindness, culture, conservation, and many other things besides. Our two groups would also perform a couple of service projects in the local communities before our group of twelve from Global Explorers went climbing Kilimanjaro.

That first morning we spent at the students' school, and they and their teacher tried teaching we Americans some Swahili phrases. The teacher and students all spoke good English, and we all shared many laughs as they attempted to teach us how to form the unfamiliar Swahili sounds. Sometimes the teacher would call on one of the Americans to say a phrase in Swahili. Then when we said it, she would ask, "Are you sure?" Quite often, we second-guessed ourselves. These question sessions often ended in fits of hysterical laughter.

After an hour or more of Swahili training, we all got back onto the buses and went to the Museum of Natural History and visited the taxidermy portion. There we listened to a man tell us about African wildlife conservation efforts. He showed us how animals were made into "trophies," as he called them. We walked around and looked at and touched animals such as goats, antelope, buffalo, snakes, and tortoises.

I was walking with my Tanzanian partner, Dorene, and a young blind Tanzanian boy. The boy asked if he could feel my cane, which I was carrying and using to scan the floor in front of me. He felt it and then asked me if I had a braille machine. I told him that I used one at home. And he asked if I might be able to teach him braille so that he could read someday. I felt for this young Tanzanian boy. I had to tell him that if we had more time, I might be able to teach him, but unfortunately, we did not have the time.

After visiting the Museum, we went to lunch—which was rice, meat, and vegetables—and then went back to the school to watch a video on the African Wildlife Foundation and what they were doing to conserve and preserve animal migration paths and the plains, rainforest on and around Kilimanjaro.

As we watched the video, a sighted Tanzanian student sat beside me and described what was happening. She would slip in Swahili animal names to see if I remembered any Swahili from the morning session. She'd say, "There's a tembo (elephant) walking. And a simba (lion) under a tree with her cubs."

After the video, we again got on the buses and drove to Moshi, a couple of hours away. We were joined on our bus by several Tanzanian students, and we all talked and laughed the whole way to our hotel.

Once we arrived at our hotel, we parted with the students—our rafikis (friends)—and checked in. Eric and Casey handed out room assignments. Brad and I took our stuff to our room, set off from the main part of the hotel building. Walking in, I immediately thought the hotel room was probably the smallest I ever stayed. It was about twelve feet by twelve feet. Two single beds were wedged together with a nightstand on either side. There was a small, twelve-inch television in the corner and a tiny bathroom with no hot water in the shower.

Brad and I shifted the beds a few inches apart and arranged our stuff the best we could. We then went to dinner, where we learned that everyone's rooms were large and comfortable. "Man, it's like we got the servants' quarters," Brad said.

A Day of Research

The following morning, we rejoined our Tanzanian counterparts. Anna, whose flight had canceled the morning we all met in Detroit, arrived the previous night. Our group was now complete.

Together our two groups traveled a couple of hours toward the Tanzania and Kenya border. We arrived at the farm of a young man named Muhammad, who could not have been more than seventeen or eighteen years old. We learned about how to analyze the soil of the farm. We examined the contents of the soil, determining how much was silt, sand, or clay. We dug several holes about three feet deep and viewed the different soil layers.

Then after washing our hands in the nearby stream and enjoying a boxed lunch, we discussed soil conservation and ways Muhammad could improve the amount of crops he produced. We then drove up to the top of a hill right on the Tanzania and Kenya border to see if we could spot the elephants that sometimes frequented the area.

However, the large, gray-skinned, floppy-eared, and long-nosed animals didn't show. We got back on the bus and drove back to Moshi, where our groups parted again.

While we were waiting for dinner, we practiced our guiding skills. We did it in the form of a game where we separated into two teams. A member from each team was blindfolded, then two Beanie Babies were tossed onto the lawn of the hotel. The two groups had to direct the blindfolded person to a Beanie Baby, and then we had to tag the other blindfolded person with the Beanie Baby. This game, of course, ended with everyone rolling on the ground laughing as we resorted to crazy methods of trying to tag each other. We would trip over our own feet as we tried dodging away from our opponent, throwing the Beanie Babies in vain attempts to tag them out from a distance. It was, again, with smiles and laughter that we ended our day looking forward to the next.

Hospital, Mweka, and Msinga

The smell of coffee permeated the air of the bus as we drove through a large plantation. We were en route to the local hospital to learn about eye procedures and to visit AIDS patients.

Once we arrived, I talked with the Tanzanians' teacher for the blind and visually impaired. She asked me all kinds of questions about my blindness and the types of technology I used to do my schoolwork. And I described to her the various computer programs I used to scan and read print documents and change them from print to braille. Then she told me about the limited supplies they had. The school had very few Perkins braillers, a standard piece of equipment for any blind student in the US—and they also had limited computer access. I again felt for these kind people. All they wanted was some help, and they weren't getting it from their government. It made me realize how very fortunate we are in the U.S. After chatting with the teacher for a while; I listened as we walked around the hospital. We visited an eye doctor who told us about the cataract epidemic in Tanzania. He told us how they prescribed glasses to patients and how the German and other governments donated most eyeglasses.

We then visited AIDS patients and told them how sorry we were for them and hoped they would recover someday. After this, we stopped at the hospital cafe for tea. Then it was off to the Mweka Wildlife College.

Here we ate lunch and visited more taxidermy rooms. We viewed stuffed birds of all sizes and colors. We went into one room with all kinds of shells and sea animal skeletons. In one room, I touched the skull of a crocodile, and in another, I stood next to the leg bone of a small elephant. This bone was almost as thick as my torso and about as tall as me—more than five-and-a-half feet tall. I wondered what it would be like to stand next to an actual elephant.

After the Mweka Wildlife College, we went to the village of Msinga —a small community outside of Moshi. At this point, Eric was getting a little antsy. We arrived at the village at 4 o'clock, and we were supposed to have been there at 1. We'd spent longer at the hospital and college than anticipated. We'd be leaving for Kilimanjaro the next day, and we all still had to pack and get a good night's sleep.

However, as we pulled into the village, we received one of the warmest and friendliest greetings ever. Village elders walked among us, shaking our hands, and kids around our age high-fived and shook our hands. They escorted us to a large circle of chairs, and the villagers put on a series of outstanding traditional song and dance performances. They sang about the deadly AIDS epidemic, nature, love, and a better future. Several were Maasai war dances. These, in particular, sent chills racing up and down my spine.

They say that during World War II, Adolf Hitler's troops hesitated and even retreated when the Maasai warriors confronted them during the conquest of Africa. And as we watched and listened, I completely understood why the Germans and Italians could have fled. These teenagers performing for us were leaping high, twirling spears, and shouting in eerie voices.

The performance that was my personal favorite was a teenage boy who sang and played a traditional African drum. He beat out complex rhythms and sang with a soft cadence that sounded mournful yet hopeful. And although I couldn't understand the words of his song, it left me and many others mesmerized.

After the performances, we helped the community members make a feast of meats, fruits, and vegetables. We talked about the importance of fuel-efficient stoves. We even saw several examples of more fuel-efficient stoves than the traditional way of building a bonfire. Initially, we had intended to build some fuel-efficient stoves with the community, but time was running out.

We sat at picnic tables and enjoyed the feast we helped to prepare. I ate fried plantains and carrots, chicken and beef, and many other delicious foods besides.

Then we gathered with the students we'd been with the last three days, and we said our goodbyes. We shook hands and hugged the people we had quickly befriended. We wished them well in their future schooling and endeavors. And they wished us well in return. Many of them gave us gifts of shell-decorated bracelets or necklaces. We felt terrible that we couldn't give them anything. But Global Explorers had arranged to have supplies donated to their school, so we felt better about that.

As we parted from our Tanzanian companions, I thought about how lucky I was. All the kids we met, among the students of the school and community of Msinga, lived in such poverty. If they had shoes, then they were often too big. Their clothes bore patches, and yet they still smiled, laughed, and kidded around with us and each other. I thought about the blind children we had met and how happy they were, even though none had canes or braillers, and there was hardly any access to computers with JAWS or other screen readers. I got to grow up surrounded by a loving and caring family that strove to make sure I had all the opportunities afforded me.

At home, I had my computer with JAWS; I had a cell phone, a soft, comfortable bed to sleep in, and the opportunity to travel to different locales worldwide and experience cultures and adventure. I was, and still am, so blessed. And my trips to Peru and Africa reinforced that.

Chapter 11

The Climb

Jambo. Jambo bwana. Habari ghani mzuri sana. Wageni. Wakaribishwa Kilimanjaro. Hakuna matata.

It was the day we'd all been anticipating. Visiting with the students was an incredible experience, but the dormant volcano that loomed high over the African plains was why we'd come here. We arrived at the Kilimanaro National Park Welcome Center and Marangu Gate—official trail entrance for the Marangu route—at 10:30 a.m. After we checked in and received all necessary permits and such Eric, Casey, and our head guide, Elias, led us to the official trailhead. It was a small wooden structure that could barely contain the group. Casey said we should say something to mark this momentous occasion before we stepped out onto the trail. And, of course, Justin summed it up perfectly. "YEEHAW!" And thus, our trek up Mt. Kilimanjaro began.

Ataana Mandara. Hakuna matata.
The first leg of our hike was through the rainforest that covers Kilimanjaro's lower slopes up to about 9,000 feet. Kilimanjaro is famous for many reasons. It's the tallest mountain in Africa. It's the world's tallest freestanding mountain—it is not part of a mountain range. And it's famous for the shrinking glacier that sits atop of it. But one of the more interesting facts about Kilimanjaro is that it's the only place on Earth where you can pass through five distinctive bio/vegetation zones: plains, rainforest, heath and moorland, desert, and arctic.

Having driven through the plains and up the mountain, we started our climb in the rainforest. We were climbing the Marangu Route. This route is the easiest up Kilimanjaro and has some rather luxurious accommodations along the way. For these reasons, westerners have dubbed it the "Coca-Cola Route." Initially, we wanted to climb the

Macham—or Whiskey—Route, which is longer and harder with more elevation changes and fewer luxuries. But our guide service was convinced that our four climbers with "vision issues," Alysha, Terry, Justin, and myself—would struggle mightily and possibly have to be rescued from higher up on the mountain. They said they would only take us up the Marangu Route. We grudgingly went along.

As we trekked through the rainforest, I noticed the path we walked upon was smooth, with only an occasional root or drainage ditch to step over. Not exactly the rugged, rocky terrain of the Peruvian Andes. Tall, moss-covered trees rose on either side of us. Safari ants rushed to and fro on the ground and up the trunks of trees. Occasionally we'd hear the cry of a bird or screech of a blue-back monkey.

At one point, we stopped and looked up. The small two-feet tall furry creatures surrounded us. Charlotte, in particular, was excited to see the monkeys. So much so that she took a total of twenty-six pictures during this short, monkey-watching break.

While Charlotte, and everyone else, was snapping a couple of photos, Justin casually said, "There's a monkey sitting on a branch directly over Max's head. If that thing takes a dump, at least it'll land on him."

Brad and I were moving briskly and efficiently along the path. Brad would say, "Up," and I'd take a step up onto a root or rock. Then he'd say, "Over," and I'd step over a ditch. Then "Up and over" to indicate I needed to step high and forward at the same time. My trekking poles swung easily in front of my boots, tapping rocks or roots that I needed to avoid. I followed the jingle of the bells that were attached to the wrist loops of Brad's poles.

Before long, the scenery around us began to change. The trees progressively got shorter and thinner. More and more scrub bushes appeared. Then suddenly, we seemed to walk out of the forest and into an entirely different world. We'd reached the heath and moorlands. Tiny feather-like plants of heather with sweet smells and tiny scrub bushes were everywhere. And it was here that we reached our first luxurious accommodation—Mandara Hut.

Mandara consisted of a series of wooden huts, including one for dining with large tables and benches and one for a bathroom lined with deep holes along each side. Thin board walls separated the holes, and privacy was then achieved by closing and latching a flimsy wooden door. Going into the bathrooms was a highly unpleasant experience. Stepping in through the front door, I immediately felt a wave of heat smack me, and I staggered out, clutching my nose and mouth to avoid breathing in the foul odor of human waste. Many of us avoided the bathrooms and preferred finding a rock or bush to hide behind.

There were also a large number of sleeping huts scattered across the cleared-out area. Brad, Justin, Terry, and I were put together in one hut. The sleeping huts were small, with four beds. One bed was on each side of the door, and then there were two stacked on top of each other, bunk-bed style, straight across from the door. Terry got the top bunk, I took the one right under him, and Brad and Justin each took the ones along the hut's sides. Standing up in the hut, I had to avoid knocking my head on the wooden beam with nails driven into it for hanging things that stretched from one wall to the other.

Before it was time to eat dinner, our guides, Elias and John, took several of us on a short little hike to Mawenzi Crater: a large pit named for one of the three peaks of Kilimanjaro. It was several hundred feet deep with steep sides and surrounded by the scrub bushes and heather.

We then hiked back and ate a dinner consisting of soup, meat, rice, and vegetables—in the dining hut. This would be our standard dinner throughout the rest of the trip. There were also always tins of tea and cocoa on every table. The hut was noisy as we weren't the only people climbing the mountain. Languages of all sorts crashed upon my ears. English dominated, but there was also French, German, Swiss, and Norwegian. Our group of American teenagers became friendly with a group of New Zealanders who seemed to share our same sense of humor. We'd run into this group from time to time over the next several days.

We all hit the hay early. Even though we'd only hiked for about four hours that day, we'd gained around 3,000 feet of elevation. We needed our sleep because we'd be hiking further up the mountain the next day and gaining more than 3,000 feet of elevation gain.

Ataana Horombo. Hakuna matata.

Terry was the first to wake up, but not knowing whether something was on the floor in the space where he could jump down, he called Justin in a whisper. "Hey, Tex. Am I clear to jump down?"

Justin looked up and said, "No, Terry, move left." Terry moved a little left. "More," Justin said.

Terry kept moving left until he touched the wall. "Here?" he asked. "Yup. Go ahead and jump," said Justin.

"But if I jump here, I'll land on Brad," Terry pointed out. "I know," Justin said matter of factly.

Brad's head buried in his fleece jacket, which he was using as a pillow. But we could all still hear him sleepily say, "DICK!"

We laughed, and Terry hopped down, managing not to land on Brad, and we all started to get up and get ready. Our objective for the day was Horombo Hut, located at 12,340 feet—a little more than halfway up the mountain.

After a breakfast of chokemeal, eggs, and tube steak, we put on some fleece and rain layers as there was a slight, chilly rain falling. We began hiking uphill. Before long, the misty rain had stopped, and we were taking off our rain jackets and pants. Then not long after that, we stripped off our fleece layers. The day was warming up quickly, and by lunch, we were all in T-shirts.

We ate lunch around an elevation of 11,000 feet. We ate ham sandwiches, chips, apples, and candy. The luxuries of hiking Kilimanjaro didn't stop at the relatively secure wooden huts with mattresses, cooked meals, and occasional soft drinks at camps like Mandara.

Porters would race past us throughout the day, carrying heavy loads of duffle bags and supplies further up the mountain. Our guides, Elias and John, hiked with us, showing us the way, pointing out different landmarks and features of the mountain. The trail was smooth, and the scenery was beautiful. I breathed deeply, smelling flowers, heather, and grasses. The bells attached to the backpack of my fellow hikers jingled merrily, the cool touch of the high-altitude air and breezes shifted past my skin, and the cheerful greetings of "Mambo!" from passing porters made the trek quite enjoyable.

Thoughts of danger and past mountaineering accidents were far from my mind. I was in good shape and was feeling strong. All we carried were light daypacks with extra layers, rain gear, water, and a few snacks.

After lunch, we climbed over a series of hills. We figured that Horombo Hut couldn't be too far ahead since we had eaten lunch at 11,000 feet, but we would climb steeply uphill and then see another hill slightly higher across the way that we needed to top. Max, Brad, Justin, John, and I were all in the lead group. We were cruising. We almost seemed to be jogging up the hills as John taught us songs the porters sang to keep them in step and high spirits as they ran up and down the mountain, shuttling loads for all the tourists. John would sing the verses and chorus, and we'd all join in when we felt we had the hang of it.

"*Jambo. Jambo bwana. Habari ghani mzuri sana. Wageni. Wakaribishwa Kilimanjaro. Hakuna matata. Ata Mandara. Hakuna matata. Ataana Horombo. Hakuna matata. Ataana Kibo. Hakuna matata. Ataana Gilman's. Hakuna matata. Ataana Uhuru. Hakuna matata. Jambo. Jambo bwana. Habari ghani mzuri sana. Wageni. Wakaribishwa Kilimanjaro. Hakuna matata.*"

Eventually, we paused at the top of one particularly long hill and looked back the way we'd come. There was nobody in sight. We perched on some large rocks next to the trail and waited. Brad, who had paused at a stream at the base of the hill, caught up to us, and then we waited for fifteen or twenty minutes before Eric, Terry, and several others joined us. John told us that Horombo was still a good step ahead of us and that we should hurry if we wanted to reserve a couple of huts. Max, Brad, Justin, John, and I shouldered our daypacks and sped off down the backside of the hill and then up the next hill. It was tough going. While the trail was relatively smooth, the constant up and down, rolling terrain wore on my feet and legs. By the top of the fifth or sixth hill, we could finally see camp after our last rest.

Down one last slope, we trekked and up the longest and steepest slope of the day. Then, finally, we dropped our packs and popped a squat on some rocks as John went to sign us in and reserve a hut for our group.

Horombo Hut sat atop a rocky slope. Buildings were spaced randomly in the flattest spots possible. There were fewer buildings here than at Mandara, but the buildings were also larger at Horombo. When we received our hut assignment, it was a trek just to get through camp. We stepped onto rocks, over rocks, and around rocks before finally reaching the door to the hut.

The sleeping huts were two-sided. Each side had six beds. We all tossed our stuff onto our chosen bunks, and before long, Eric came in to tell us that one guy would have to go over to the girl's side of the hut. Seven guys and five girls didn't make perfect sleeping arrangements, but we worked it out. Brad, Max, Justin, Eric, Ryan, and I bunked on one side while Terry went over to the girl's side to bunk with Casey, Anna, Jill, Charlotte, and Alysha.

After dinner, we gathered on the boy's side of the hut for what we called "Story Time." Casey had brought along a book written by a man who had grown up in a Maasai Warrior village. Each night we gathered to read a chapter or two in the book. We learned about all the Maasai traditions still practiced in many remote villages. I listened as Brad read a chapter aloud about someone in the village known as the "Pinching Man." Parents sent their children to him for punishment. Then Anna read a chapter about the Maasai schooling traditions. Each family was required to have at least one member of the family attend school. The family member had to be at least eight years old. The author of the book was six at the time but wanted to go to school and volunteered. The authorities who came to the house to test the boy had a strange way of telling whether he was eight. They made him stretch his right arm above his head and then reach over the top of his head to touch his left ear. If he touched it, he was eight, and if not, then he was younger and could not attend, and therefore his older brother would need to attend school. He touched his ear and was permitted to go to school.

After reading a while, we all retired to our beds. I fell asleep almost instantly and didn't wake until the alarm went off and it was time for breakfast.

Acclimatization Day

Over chokemeal, eggs, tube steak, coffee and tea, I listened as Charlotte recounted her nighttime adventure. She had woken up in the middle of the night and found a mouse calmly snoozing on her pillow. She shrieked and leaped across onto Anna's bunk. The entire girls' hut woke up along with a few guys, but I had slept through it and not heard a thing.

Then we went back to the huts and packed a daypack. We weren't going to make upward progress that day. We were going to use the day to acclimatize to the higher elevations. But on Kilimanjaro, an acclimatization day means being lazy. We planned on going on a short hike to view some of the sights around camp.

Somewhere around 25,000 people attempt to summit Kilimanjaro every year, and about 15,000—on average—reach the true summit, Uhuru Peak, at 19,340 feet. Kilimanjaro is not a technical climb. It does not require any special tools, equipment, or even a ton of experience to reach the top. The reason 10,000 people give up and turn around before the summit is not fatigue, injury, or difficulty; it's the altitude.

As you climb higher up a mountainside, the oxygen-rich air becomes thinner. There's less oxygen getting into the blood and to the brain, which can cause headaches, nausea and make people tire at much faster rates. This phenomenon is known as Acute Mountain Sickness—more commonly called altitude sickness.

Climbers do their best to prevent AMS by doing cardiovascular training to boost their red blood cells, which carry oxygen from our lungs to the different parts of our bodies.

As we get higher in elevation, the air becomes dryer and colder, causing the body to use more moisture and the blood to thicken, leading to dehydration and attributes to AMS. We drank four or more liters—roughly about a gallon—of water a day to prevent this.

One of the many beautiful things about our bodies is that they adapt to the environment and situation. Thus, the acclimatization day. The idea was to do some light hiking and let our bodies adapt to the lower oxygen levels to be stronger for the summit push. Thus, we set off on our day trip to Zebra Rocks. This rock formation was a large boulder that had stripes, similar to those of a zebra. The stripes developed from the water that dripped down the face of the boulder and stained it darker over time.

After checking out Zebra Rocks—or Wamba wa Pundamilia (Zebra Rocks, in Swahili), like Justin, Terry, and I called them—we hiked around, and Elias told us about the geologic history of Kilimanjaro. We had known that it was a volcano. Elias told us to pick up several different rocks. There were rocks everywhere and of all shapes, sizes, and colors. Touching the different rocks, we noticed that some were jagged and rough, while others seemed smooth as glass. Terry tapped his trekking pole against one rock, and it seemed to "tink," as though he had tapped a piece of glass. Elias explained that when Kilimanjaro last erupted, the lava had settled on different parts of the mountain. The roughness or smoothness was dependent on how quickly or slowly the lava cooled.

After this, we hiked for a bit longer and then headed back to the huts to nap before dinner. We again readout of our book about more of the Maasai traditions, and then it was off to bed.

The Alpine Desert and Kibo Hut
Ataana Kibo. Hakuna matata.

"Holy shit! That's a huge ass hill!" Brad said as we hiked.

We had started hiking at 8:30 in the morning and planned to stop for lunch around 12:30. We'd been hiking uphill; then the ground leveled off. We were now in what is called the Alpine Desert. The conditions were dry, rocky, dusty, and windy. The wind blew from higher on the mountain, and dust seemed to coat our faces, mouths, and noses. We climbed steadily up the "Huge ass hill" that Brad had mentioned to me. It was a long, steep ascent. The wind whipped dust into our faces, and there was nothing green to be found for miles around. All there was to see were rocks, sand, and each other.

We passed the time by playing word and memory games. Casey kept everyone entertained with jokes and riddles.

Finally, we reached the crest of the hill and came in sight of our lunch spot.

We hiked downhill and set up shop in a mini boulder field. Many of us sought out places where we could get sunlight and a blockage from the wind. The temperature was dropping the higher we got, and the wind was persistent. We laughed as a mouse jumped into Casey's lunchbox, pooped, and then hopped back out again. We watched as some birds wheeled overhead, rising on the updrafts. And then it was time to make the final push toward Kibo Hut.

Many people bundled up in fleece jackets and extra layers. We all had sunglasses to try and keep the dust from getting into our eyes. People were starting to feel the effects of the altitude. Headaches, nausea, coughing were all present. Anna and Alysha had been fighting slight colds for the past couple of days, and the dust and higher altitude were not helping. With the dry air and dust swirling around, I was starting to cough.

Max and I were at the front of the group, and we trudged into the wind. I had to keep my head down; otherwise, the wind would blow and moan in my ears, making it was difficult to hear the bells swinging from Max's pack. I hummed the porters' songs to myself as I continued putting one foot in front of the other and continued working my way uphill. Eventually, Max saw a distant, hazy smudge atop the next long rise.

Kibo Hut was much smaller than Mandara and Horombo. There were four buildings. A couple of large sleeping huts were the most solidly built structures we had yet seen on the mountain, a couple of huts for the porters, and an outhouse. The hut that we made our home was large. The building was almost like a little house on the mountain. Thick plaster walls kept out the night chill and wind, and the dining room was just down the hall from our room. In total, the hut contained three or four bedrooms in addition to the dining room. Our room was the largest, with six sets of bunk beds, and we all bunked together at Kibo.

I occupied a top bunk right next to the door with Ryan directly beneath me.

For the most part, we always laughed and joked. However, during the last push to Kibo, everyone was quiet, concentrating on just getting to the hut. We were now all ensconced in our beds, and apart from the occasional cough, all I heard was heavy breathing. We were all tired.

We were at 15,500 feet, and our bodies knew it. Many of us were coughing and tired. Hardly anyone wanted to do anything more than sleep.

We dragged ourselves out of bed to eat dinner and then fell right back into bed. No one was up to reading from the book we'd all been so interested in since the beginning of our trek up Kilimanjaro. We just slept and conserved as much of our strength and energy for the next night's summit bid.

Rest Day

The day after we arrived at Kibo was a rest day. Those of us that were up to it went for a short acclimatization hike up to 16,500 feet. It took us a couple of hours as we intentionally slowed our pace way down. Then it was back down to the hut for lunch and back to the room to sleep.

Given that we would be leaving that night at midnight for the summit, Eric's order/advice of the day was "Get as much sleep as possible."

Chapter 12

Summit Fever

Ataana Gilman's. Hakuna matata.

    We stood under the immense sweep of the open sky. Brad looked up and saw the headlamps of climbers—including Ryan and Casey, who would set out an hour earlier—bobbing up and down looking like moving stars in the heavens. We'd all gotten up around 11:30 p.m. and ate a small breakfast. We put on our layers—it was in the high 20s at best—and packed a few snacks in our packs. Now it was time to summit or plummet.

    Justin and I had long planned for him to lead me on this momentous night. However, as we stood outside with only the light of the stars and our headlamps to see by, Justin turned to me and said, "K Coon, I can barely see a thing. So, there's no way I can guide anyone tonight."

    "Look, bro," I said, "I understand. Don't sweat it. Let's just make the summit." I gave my bells to Max, and it was go-time.

    We set off, slowly, uphill. Charlotte had woken up not feeling good at all. She managed to join us for breakfast and hiked with us for around half an hour. But once that half-hour passed, Charlotte had to admit that she just wasn't up to making it all the way. She turned around and headed back down to Kibo, accompanied by one of the porters. We were all sad to see her go. One of our primary goals had been to get everyone to the top. However, the mountains hold no prejudice and have no mercy. We pushed on.

    Max and I took up the group's rear, forcing us to slow our pace and not gallivant off up the mountain. We would come to Kilimanjaro as a team, and we all wanted to summit as a team. Max gave me a cinnamon-flavored toothpick, and the sharp, sweet taste of cinnamon helped keep me awake and alert.

I got into a rhythm of stepping and breathing. Deep, slow breaths. In through the nose and out through the mouth. Step, step, breathe. Step, step, breathe.

Every forty-five minutes to an hour, we stopped to drink water and rest for a few minutes. During one of these water breaks, Max looked up and described the pure white bands of stars that made up the Milky Way spreading out in a continuous line across the black of the night sky. I was awed and humbled to be a witness to such beauty. I could feel the bite of the cold through my layers and the steep, slippery scree beneath my boots. The slope that we kicked our feet into was about the steepness of a Black Diamond ski slope. And all the while, every step, every breath brought us closer and closer to the distant bands of snow that our group could glimpse.

We caught up to Ryan and Casey around 17,000 feet. Ryan had wanted to set out early since he knew he had been moving slow. He wanted to be able to summit with the team and not slow the entire group down. Even though Ryan was moving slow, the rest of us were too, and we all fell into step and climbed steadily higher.

Then around 17,300 feet, Eric brought the group to a stop. "Guys, Ryan's decided to head down. I've already summitted this mountain twice, and Global Explorers' policy is that we cannot leave so many people behind. Since Casey hasn't summitted this mountain yet, she'll go with you guys to the summit. And I'll go down to be with Ryan and Charlotte."

Ryan would tell me several days later—as we hiked down together through the heath and moorlands—that he felt he could have made the summit but didn't think that he would have the strength to get back down. As hard as this is for many people to imagine, Ryan made the right decision. Many a climber has given everything they had to reach the summit to discover that the summit was only halfway. My ski guide, Dave Gadbaw, always advised me as we approached the end of a day on the slopes, "Always quit one run before you're done." You still need strength and energy to get back home. The same rule applies when climbing. Getting to the top is pointless if you can't get down. So, Ryan headed down.

Eric came around to each of us individually and spoke words of encouragement. When he reached me, he hugged me and said, "Be strong, Kyle. I know you can make it."

Eric had been our team leader from the beginning. We all looked up to him. No matter what the situation, he always seemed to have an answer. He took time out of each day to speak with everyone and become a role model. Now he was telling me to be strong and that I could make it. And I knew I could.

I hugged him back and said, "Thanks, Eric." Then we turned our sights upward and onward. Eric stood below and watched as we climbed up toward the summit. Then he turned around and headed down.

Before long, we started scrambling up and through a rock field. We'd left the scree slope behind and were stepping up, onto, around, and over rocks of all sizes. I was using my hands almost as much as my feet. Anna, Jill, Alysha, and Casey stopped to rest for a minute and Max, and I went ahead of them, staying right behind Brad, Terry, and Justin. Then Alysha leaned over and deposited her offering of stomach contents to the mountain gods. Even though she had just hurled, and her voice sounded scratchy and gravelly, she said, "I'm fine. Let's keep going."

Terry was also starting to struggle. Brad and Justin encouraged him. "Come on, Terry," Justin said, "I can see the sign at Gilman's Point."

And then we were there. Not at the summit, but Gilman's point about 1,000 feet below the summit. We all celebrated by plopping down on some rocks, drinking water, taking a group photo, and taking a fifteen-minute rest.

Ataana Gilman's. Hakuna matata.

Terry was sitting with his head in his hands. "I don't know if I can go much farther," he said.

I patted him on the back and gave him two tablets of Advil. "You can make it, man! We're almost there," I encouraged. Then it was time to get moving.

The sun had been slowly rising higher and higher over the peak painting the sky with brilliant hues of all sorts. It warmed our faces and made us feel alive. I had a slight headache but felt super strong.

Max guided me down a short slope, then around a bend to the left, and the world seemed to fall away on my right. We could peer down into the caldera—the crater at the top of Kilimanjaro from where lava spewed many, many years ago. Now it was filled with snow and rock. A solid wall of rock was to my left.

Max passed my bells to Elias, and the two of us took the lead. We walked through a trench cut into the snow. Elias was jingling the bells so enthusiastically that they started to give Casey, who was hiking right behind me, a headache. She asked Elias to tone down the jingling just a bit. He did, to my delight as much as everyone else's. It is difficult listening to the shrill ringing of bells at 19,000 feet of elevation.

We climbed higher and higher. We stepped out of the trench and onto a steep snowy slope. Elias looked up and said he could see the sign that's perched atop the mountain.

Then I felt the ground level out under my feet. Elias linked his arm with mine. And the two of us walked across a wide-open expanse—about 200 feet—to the sign that sits atop Mt Kilimanjaro. Elias placed my hand on the sign and said, "Welcome to the top of Africa."

The sign read, "You are at Uhuru Peak. 5895 meters. The highest point in Africa."

It was 7:30 A.M. on June 25, 2007. I was fifteen years old and had just summitted Mt Kilimanjaro.

I felt my throat start to swell and moisture in the corners of my eyes. And then I heard Justin, Brad, and Terry right behind me. "Here, Terry. Come touch this sign," Justin was saying. Then there was a thump and laughter. "I didn't mean walk into it," Justin said.

"I found it," Terry said.

Then we were all there: Casey, Anna, Alysha, Jill, Brad, Justin, Max, Terry, Elias, John, and a whole host of other porters who had trekked up with us. For some of them, it was their first time atop Kilimanjaro, too. We all hugged, high-fived, whooped, and yeehawed.

Casey pulled out the two-way radio we had brought up with us to let Eric know when we'd made it, and she triumphantly told him. And "Congratulations!" was the excited reply.

We took picture after picture. I sat with my arms around Terry, on my left, and Justin, on my right. The three of us had initially hatched this idea, so we made sure to get a picture together. Everyone got a group shot with their cameras.

And then all that was left to do was head down. But before we left, Justin, Terry, and I really needed to take a piss. We walked a little ways away from the sign and pissed on the roof of Africa. Yeah, we conquered the mountain!

Power Sliding

It took us about an hour and a half or two to get down from the summit, past Gilman's Point and through the rock fields below Gilman's. Once we did, Max looked around to make sure there weren't any dangerous rocks. Then with a whoop, he shouted, "Let's go!" And we started hauling ass downhill.

The scree fields above Kibo Hut that took us hours to climb up took no time to get down. Max and I'd run, taking giant plunging steps, and then we would drop into ski position and let our feet slide and make ski turns in the loose sand. John and Brad were right there with us. We were all hooting and hollering. Justin, Terry, and Elias were not far behind, and the girls were all a little bit farther back. Dust caked my face, inside my mouth and nose, stuck to my shirt and pants, and stuck in my hair.

Before we knew it, we blinked, and there was Eric, grinning from ear to ear and carrying a jar of Pringles as he hiked up toward us. Not far behind him was Kibo Hut. It wasn't even lunchtime yet.

Once we arrived at the hut, a porter presented us with glasses of passion fruit juice—what a tasty beverage after summiting a mountain. Then we ate lunch, took a nap, packed our gear, and started heading down the mountain.

Down, Down, Down

We left Kibo Hut around 4 p.m. and made it down to Horombo in time for a late dinner. We tumbled into bed.

The following day began with the crowing of a rooster that was Eric's phone alarm he'd set to ensure we could get up and get moving on time. Over breakfast, we learned that one of our porters had developed pulmonary edema. This condition is when the lungs fill with fluid and is caused by ascending a mountain too quickly. The quickest and most straightforward remedy is descent to lower elevations and more oxygen. A few porters put together a stretcher, put the afflicted porter on it, made him breathe bottled oxygen, and raced down the mountain. Elias, as head guide, was responsible for taking care of the porters, so he went ahead with them.

The rest of us began our descent much slower. We hiked down to Mandara Hut and had lunch, consisting of sandwiches, pizza, bananas, oranges, and soft drinks. It was beyond good to have a Coke after a week of almost nothing but water. Then we paired off again and started working our way down to the Marangu Gate.

Eric raced on ahead of everyone to make sure he paid and tipped all the porters. Brad was guiding me as we hiked speedily down through the rainforest. Occasionally we would pass other hikers going in the opposite direction toward Mandara. As Brad and I hiked, I couldn't help but marvel at the silence around us. If it had not been for the bells that Brad was ringing, the sound of his voice giving me directions, and the crunch of our boots on slippery rocks, roots, and gravel, there would have been nothing. Each time we stopped to take a drink of water, we would hear the sounds of wildlife. Birds chirped, and monkeys cackled, but even though Brad strained his eyes in all directions, we couldn't catch a glimpse of them, even though it sounded like they were no more than a few feet away.

We eventually reached the gate and found Eric. We waited a while for the rest of the group to arrive and then piled onto the bus, where the ride's highlight was us singing celebratory traditional Swahili songs about Kilimanjaro. These were the same songs that John and Elias taught to us on the mountain. Several of our porters had hung around and waited to ride back to town with us. The happy and excited sounds of everyone singing brought a smile to my face that stayed for days.

Jambo. Jambo bwana.
Habari ghani
Mzuri sana.
Wageni.
Wakaribishwa Kilimanjaro.
Hakuna matata.
Ataana Mandara.
Hakuna matata.
Ataana Horombo.
Hakuna matata.
Ataana Kibo.
Hakuna matata.
Ataana Gilman's.
Hakuna matata.
Ataana Uhuru.
Hakuna matata.
Jambo. Jambo bwana.
Habari ghani
Mzuri sana.
Wageni.
Wakaribishwa Kilimanjaro.

Hakuna matata. Uhuru. Freedom?

The small 1,000-foot-tall peak that sits atop Kilimanjaro bears the name Uhuru—which, in Swahili, means Freedom. I think mountains are all about freedom. In the U.S., sometimes words like teamwork and freedom are thrown around with impunity. It took many years to love and appreciate the freedoms that I enjoy as an American citizen. The older I got, and the more I learned, the more I realized how blessed I am.

The day after we returned to Arusha, we walked around the local market to buy souvenirs. We enjoyed haggling over prices for items such as hand-carved drums, jewelry, animal carvings, decorative spears, and other such knickknacks.

Eric was chatting with a local vendor and told her that he had just returned from leading a group of American teenagers, some of whom were totally blind, up Kilimanjaro. The woman didn't believe him at first, and Eric promised her that he was telling the truth. He then came and found Terry and me and asked us to meet the woman. We did, and she clasped our hands, saying, "God bless you! God bless you! You are so amazing." Other vendors heard and came to meet us.

Terry and I were overwhelmed. We had just climbed a mountain. Okay, it was awesome, but we were not the first, nor would we be the last to do it. However, these people thought we were so amazing. We'd had a dream that was born from our trip to Peru the year before. And we had merely followed the path that led us to this place. We had the freedom to make choices and decisions that would positively or negatively affect our lives. That freedom is within each of us as humans. Sometimes it takes people longer to realize that it is there. Sometimes governments and administrations try to suppress it. But it's there.

George Leigh Mallory, who famously died while trying to be the first man to climb Mt. Everest, was once asked why he wanted to climb the mountain. He replied, "Because it's there." Erik Weihenmayer pointed out in his book that the unspoken part of Mallory's quote was that "We are here."

The mountains, for me, opened up worlds of opportunity. Trekking through the jungles of Peru and walking across the glacier atop Kilimanjaro was only the beginning of a long journey.

I realize that the freedom to follow the path of my life is within me. It's up to me to strive for and reach those goals—known and unknown. But I could not have gotten this far without the help of my family, teachers, friends, and teammates.

Peru showed me that the destination did not matter as much as the journey along the path we take to get there. Furthermore, Kilimanjaro reinforced how blessed I am to have the freedom to follow and enjoy that path. However, despite the excitement, adventure, and sense of wonder those places provided me, there was much more to come.

Chapter 13

True Companion

Never Smile at a Crocodile

Mountain climbing is all about teamwork, and teamwork is about building trust and rapport. Before and after I summited a mountain, I had a different set of furry teachers that helped me learn how to develop those traits.

When I was a toddler, between the ages two and three, my older sister, Cassandra, and I were a bit obsessed with the Disney movie Peter Pan. We must have watched it a hundred times. We enamored with the thought of never growing up and playing all day on an enchanted island, a common game we played in the front yard of our house in Orange Park, FL. The game had us spreading our arms wide, running all over the grass, pretending we were flying through Neverland.

However, there were occasions, which came on abruptly, that had me calling to Cassandra, "Come on, Wendy. Follow me," and with arms flapping wildly, my little legs propelled me into the safety and solitude of our back yard. The fear fueled by the sight of the neighbor's Golden Retriever, who would stroll out of his front door and lumber down his driveway, no doubt attracted by the squealing blonde children across the street. To me, this dog looked like a giant and as ferocious as the crocodile Peter Pan battled off Captain Hook's boat.

Cassandra always followed me on that flight, and to this day, I believe she was as scared of the dog as I was, though she won't admit it. Neither one of us can recall the dog's name. He wasn't mean and never hurt anyone. He was just big. And it fueled a fear of dogs in me at a very young age.

Contributing to my fear was the fact that we didn't have a dog as a family pet. My Dad had grown up on a farm, and animals were not pets. They were food. They certainly never came into the house.

I was also afraid of the Meehan's two dachshunds, Sugar and Oscar. The Meehans lived next door to us. They were small dogs, but I wouldn't go near them, even though I played with Andrew Meehan all the time. Andy's dad was one of those big goofy dads, and he kept encouraging me to get close to Sugar and Oscar. He would hold Sugar, the smaller of the two, and call me over. "Go ahead, pet her, Kyle," he would encourage me. One day, I did. She wagged her tail. Mr. Meehan kept doing that—holding Sugar and gently encouraging me to pet her—each time I went to their house. As I got braver, he would tell me to stick my finger in her mouth and feel her teeth. I did and never lost a finger. It was a breakthrough, you could say.

After that, I began to come in contact with more dogs, and they were all nice. Of course, I am growing, too, and getting taller and bigger than the dogs. In my vision classes at school, there were storybooks about blind children with guide dogs, so I was familiar with the notion that dogs could help blind people. But until I lost that fear, I didn't picture myself with a guide dog. How short-sighted of me. Because once I lost my sight, I thought about it all the time.

Puppy Love

The first guide dog I ever met was Seego, Erik Weihenmayer's German Shepherd. In all the books I read before my surgery, the stories always made a point about how special guide dogs were, and other people couldn't pet them or interact for fear of distracting them from their job. So, when I met Erik at age seven, and he asked me if I wanted to pet Seego, I knew it was a big deal. He took off Seego's harness—an important signal to a guide dog—and said, "He's ready for you, Kyle." I remember the pointy ears and running my hand down his silky head and his back. Seego never flinched. It was absolutely a transitional moment in my life and my future as a blind person.

After that day, I thought about getting a guide dog all the time. I kept asking when I could get one. My parents were great about it and told me I would get one someday, but I would have to be patient. Like the character-building my Dad always told me about, this was not easy for me.

Generally, blind people do not get placed with guide dogs until around age sixteen, meaning I had a wait of about nine years from the day I met Seego. On top of that, I had never even had a dog in my house, much less by my side.

Without us kids knowing, my Mom began to work on my dad about getting a dog for the family. It would get me ready for the responsibility—feeding, walking, grooming—and it would get the family ready for having a four-legged member of our busy household.

Mom prevailed, though I am sure my Dad did not need a massive amount of persuasion. He knew a guide dog would do much for me, and he would never have wanted it any other way. But those farm roots run deep, and he just needed time to get used to the idea of a dog in the house.

One day in November, just a few days before my twelfth birthday, I was in the driveway shooting hoops with my best friend, John Norville. He was beating me, which is totally not fair since he could see the hoop. My Mom came out into the driveway, jiggling car keys, and told me to get in the car because we were running errands. She added, "John, you're coming with us. I talked to your mom."

My sisters, John, and I piled into the car, and we drove for what seemed like a longer time than usual to go to the mall or the grocery store, or Costco. But with all the chatter—and possibly bickering—in the car that none of us noticed.

Finally, the car stopped, and my sisters climb out. John grabbed my arm, leading me. He was in on it, and Kelsey knew what was going on. However, Cassandra and I were clueless—me more so since she could see where we were. It's very easy to pull off surprises on me, something my family relishes.

We were at my scout master's house, Mr. New, and they bred Labrador Retrievers. As John is guiding me, my Mom is videotaping the entire scene, and my scout master's wife, Mrs. New, said, "Hold out your hands, Kyle." And when I did, she dropped an eight-week-old black Labrador puppy into my hands.

She was my birthday present. Well, she was also Cassandra's birthday present, since our birthdays are a week apart. While I am processing the moment, I hear John's mom's voice saying, "This one's for you, John," and deposited the brother into his hands.

Talk about excitement. I couldn't believe I had a puppy. I couldn't believe my mom talked dad into it. I was too excited; I didn't even care that John got one, too.

We named her Genevieve, and we loved that dog from the moment we brought her home. John's family named her brother Cooper, and he would grow to 120 pounds compared to Genevieve's 60. As a new puppy, Genevieve had it pretty good. There were four kids in the house wanting to play with her, so she never wanted for attention. It was my job to feed her every night. My three sisters took turns taking her outside to do her business. We all took care of her, but the setup from the beginning was that I would do a bit more than my sisters to prepare me for the responsibility of my guide dog someday.

Genevieve, or Gen as we called her, was a blast. I would roll around on the floor with her, tug on a rope for endless hours, throw balls for her. She always knew where they went, which was good since I didn't. I also gave her baths—though I think I got cleaner than she did since I always wound up just as wet and soapy as she did. She had boundless energy, and so did I.

She was a great dog, the best first dog. Like my parents knew she would, Gen got me ready for the responsibility and the rewards of a guide dog.

Tap, Tap, Tapping Along

I knew I couldn't get a guide dog for four years or more after we got Gen, and that seemed like an excruciatingly long time. With my parents' guidance, I turned that lack of patience into motivation to get good at cane skills. I take that back. Not just good. Exceedingly great.

The white cane had been part of my life since before I went blind. In elementary school, I learned the elementary stuff: cane travel, learning a little bit about traffic, basic navigation. After my second eye surgery, I did use the cane—I had to. But the thing is, the easiest, fastest, and least scary way for a blind person to get around is to be lead by someone—a friend or a family member. You grab their arm or their hand; they tell you where you are, when to turn, what direction, alert you to what's in the way, and maneuver you around it. I can't speak for every blind person, but if I could have my mom take me everywhere, as a pre-teenager, that's what I would probably have chosen.

As comfortable and easy as that sounds, I knew, even as a pre-teenager, that I would never have independence that way. It wasn't reality. Would my Mom go to prom with me? Go to college? My first job? Even a stubborn adolescent, like me, knew that wasn't an option. And I did want independence. Step one was a cane. Step two would be a guide dog. I could not skip step one and go right to step two.

My Mom and sisters watched videos and read books about how to train Genevieve. They worked with her every day to teach her to heel, sit, stay and lay down. Once they had it down, they trained me. That way, we could all be consistent, which is essential when training a dog. I want to tell you I was a faster learner than Gen, but that might not be the case. However, I enjoyed the experience. Walking with her on a leash and not having her pull me all over the place, but walk calmly at my side, was an incredible feeling.

In middle school, I attacked cane skills with all my competitive spirit. Genevieve lit a fire in me to get a guide dog as soon as I could. My muses would be Theresa Drane and Karlin Michelson, orientation and mobility specialists (or O&M as us blind folks say), who also worked at Fishweir, my elementary school, and other kids around the county. From first through fifth grade, two days a week, Mrs. Drane would work with me to build a foundation and improve upon what I already knew.

Blind people use canes to find obstacles in our path, things that can trip us up. You tap, tap, tap to find the edge of the sidewalk or curb, to listen for your cane to run into a step, so you know when to step up. You can find light poles, signposts, or fire hydrants and get around them.

Using the cane, tapping, finding the obstacles became so natural to me after a while that I cannot recall how I even learned it. I kept my cane in step with my stride. While it's a great way for blind people to navigate, it's very jerky—especially for me. I'm a fast walker. Everyone tells me that, and it's just how I am. I have never learned how to slow down. And because I walk so fast, obstacles can come up on me faster than I can tap them out. I have three scars on my forehead—one very Harry Potter-like—to prove it. With my cane in hand, I walked into walls, doors, and poles, mid tap, and my Mom took me to the emergency room every time to have my head taped or stitched.

Another downfall of traveling with a cane is how the tip can catch in a sidewalk or jam into a step, abruptly stopping you and anyone behind you. People can trip over your cane, and one of my teachers in high school, drama teacher Brenda Chapman, tripped over mine in the hallway between classes and broke her arm.

While canes are great tools for the blind, they have downfalls.

Cane skills are also not enough to be truly independent. Blind people have to learn skills to navigate from one place to another. Cane skills are essential to our mobility, and it takes intensive training. Once I started high school, the talk at home of me getting a guide dog hit level three. It was time for me to step up my O&M training.

Leaving The Band of Lost Boys

I had met Karlyn Michelson, the O&M instructor for sixth grade through twelfth graders in my county when I was in sixth grade, and we began some intensive cane travel work. We would work together through my senior year of high school.

Mrs. Michelson would take me to downtown Jacksonville in her car, and we would start on a corner. She would tell me, in a running banter, things like:

"This is North Lauer, and we are about to intersect with Adams. This is the northeast corner of the intersection. On a sunny day, you can tell the position of the sun. It rises in the east and sets in the west. Where you feel it on your face tells you the direction you're heading. If you get lost and don't know where you are, feel the sun. Listen to the sound of traffic flow. In this part of town, the streets only go one way."

After walking and talking like this for a whole semester, Mrs. Michelson had taught me an entire eight-block radius in downtown Jacksonville. Then she began to test me by taking me to the major intersections, like Park Avenue and King Street, then walk me around, turning at corners, crossing streets. "Okay, Kyle," she would say. "Find your way back to Park and King." And I would tap, tap, tap, walking alone, though she was walking behind me, but a ways back so I would feel alone.

I confess it was nerve-wracking. We started this in sixth grade, and it took me a while to get comfortable with it. If Mrs. Michelson saw me start to make a wrong turn, she would step in and talk to me about the choice I made, why I made it, and then talk to me about how to read the surroundings differently next time. I did get lost in sixth grade, and I felt frustrated. But Mrs. Michelson was very patient and kept encouraging me.

For my final exam, Mrs. Michelson drove her car to a random location in downtown Jacksonville. She told me to get out of the car and find my way back to the northeast corner of Park and King. I unfolded my cane, and I took a deep breath. I felt the sun. I listened to the traffic. Two-way. I turned, and I tap, tap, tapped my way. With each block, I felt more confident because I knew where I was on the grid. Two blocks away from the goal, I imagined the theme song from Rocky playing through loudspeakers across the downtown streets. When I tapped my cane on the street sign on the northeast corner of Park and King, I was beaming. And then I heard Mrs. Michelson say, "Great job, Kyle."

I killed it.

A Dog By Any Other Name

> After World War I, Dorothy Harrison Eustis, an American, was training German Shepherd dogs in Switzerland to be guides for blinded war veterans. An article about her ground-breaking work caught the attention of Morris Frank, who was frustrated by his lack of mobility as a blind person. He wrote to Dorothy and vowed he would spread the word about these amazing dogs if she would help him. Soon, he was in Switzerland receiving training.
>
> In 1928, Morris Frank walked with his dog, Buddy, a German Shepherd, around the streets of New York, as reporters watched what Buddy was able to do for Frank.
>
> This led to the birth of The Seeing Eye, founded in 1929. It is the oldest existing guide dog school in the world. Each month, 24 students at a time visit the Morristown, N.J,. campus to receive training and their very own dog. To date, more than 15,500 specially bred and trained dogs have brought a new level of mobility, safety, and self-sufficiency to more than 8,000 blind or visually impaired men and women.
>
> The Seeing Eye holds the trademark on "The Seeing Eye," so only dogs from this organization can be called "seeing-eye dogs." All others are called guide dogs.

I read all this information on the website for The Seeing Eye after another guide dog school had rejected me. It was the same guide dog school Erik went to, and he told me to contact them after him. I was feeling pretty dejected when they said I was too young to get a dog, but I turned that energy into finding a school that would accept me.

The Seeing Eye impressed me. They had an excellent reputation. The school Erik recommended to me brought a dog to you and trained you in your surroundings. They did not come to the state of Florida, so even if they hadn't said I was too young, that wasn't an option. The Seeing Eye brought you to its campus, got to know you, and the dog breeder and trainer matched you with a dog based on both your personalities. I liked the sound of that.

I was in the middle of my junior year of high school, and I desperately wanted a dog by my senior year. Ideally, I wanted to get my dog the summer before my senior year. I knew every corridor, classroom, and hallway of the Paxon School for Advanced Studies, so navigating the school with a dog would be a piece of cake.

Having a guide dog for my senior year of high school was important to me for several reasons. I wanted to have a year with my guide dog in a place that was familiar to me. I was thinking about college. For any incoming freshman, it's stressful going to college. It's a new place; you have to figure out how to find buildings and your classes in the buildings. For a blind student, these stresses are more intense because it takes longer to figure all that out, and we need more repetition to get it down. The last thing I wanted was the stress of memorizing the layout of a campus in my mind and developing a bond with a new guide dog. Having my dog with me for my last year of high school would give us that time to get to know each other.

Once I found The Seeing Eye, I talked to my parents. They agreed it sounded like a great place, and I began the incredibly long application process. Man, they ask you a lot of questions. My height. My weight. Age of vision loss. Cause of vision loss. My experience with pets (way to go, Mom and Dad). How much mobility instruction I had (thanks, Mrs. Michelson). And I had to write a letter of self-introduction. I did it all as fast as my fingers could fly across the keyboard.

I would have to travel to Moorestown, N.J., for twenty-six days of training to be matched with my dog. I settled on summer. I would live in the dorms and work with a trainer one-on-one. This trainer would match me with my dog based on our personalities.

What was truly amazing is that for $150 I received: the dog that had received a year of training, my instruction, room, and board for twenty-six days, the harness and leashes, the air transportation to and from Morristown, and the car that picks you up at the airport. This package is such a blessing for blind people. Those services, which are invaluable, are in reach for nearly every blind person who wants them, and I hope to do all I can to spread the word about guide dog providers, so people know all they do.

I sent in my application in December of my junior year. All applications go before a Board of Directors and a selection committee. I was selected for a phone interview. I was nervous, but I must have done pretty well because a man named John came to our home to interview me in March.

As a seventeen-year-old, I hadn't figured this out, but now it seems obvious as an adult. John wanted to check out our living conditions. He wanted to make sure a dog would be in a safe and clean environment. John also walked with me, talked to me, and talked to my Mom. We talked for two and a half hours, and now I realize he was getting a feel for my personality. Was I a hot head? Was I a responsible person? I don't remember the questions he asked me, but I remember thinking he was a lovely man.

The waiting was agony. Would I be accepted? Would they think I was too young? Would I ever get a guide dog? Two weeks later, a call came from The Seeing Eye, and they said they would be happy to match me with a dog. A big fat packet arrived in the mail a week later, and I was excited. They accepted me for a summer session, and it was all final by April of my junior year of high school. Before I knew it, I was on a plane heading north to meet my guide dog.

He's Your Dog Now

What is the most essential ability a blind person must have before getting a guide dog? Walking. At least, that's the impression I got at The Seeing Eye. At least, for the first two days.

In those first two days, the twenty-four students split into groups of four. Each group had an instructor who had eight trained dogs. It's important to know that while guide dogs are bred for this purpose and screened for disposition and health issues, not every dog that goes through guide dog training will make it. Some get spooked by traffic. Some are too docile. Some are too aggressive. So, it takes a great deal of skill and dedication, and sometimes plain luck, to get a guide dog to the level of skill mastery necessary to be put into service.

In those first two days, we walked around with the instructor. They gave each student an empty harness, and they taught us how to hold it. The instructors watched how fast you walked. They taught you how to correct your dog, which is when you give a fast, quick tug on your dog's leash to let them know they have done something they shouldn't. And all the while, there was talking, lots and lots of talking. The instructors were getting to know us. My instructor was Sue McCahill. And while I walked around with my empty harness and leash, Sue would say to me: "So, Kyle, you wrestle, right? You're the captain of the high school team? How many sisters do you have? Do you like the beach? Competitive mountain climbing? That sounds interesting. Where do you want to go to college? What will be your major? How long did it take you to learn how to snow ski? What's your favorite movie? Do you have a girlfriend? What kind of music do you like? How often do you exercise?"

Banter. There was constant banter. I had no idea how important this was to the work Sue did.

In the evenings, we had sessions where we watched videos on the history of The Seeing Eye. (Yes, we watched videos. The dialog is excellent.) And I learned even more about the history and philosophies of this oldest guide dog school in the country.

Some nights, they had graduates of The Seeing Eye come and talk to us about their experiences. Graduates told us how they deal with strangers wanting to pet their guide dogs and interact with them. These scenarios would be beneficial to me. It's only natural that people want to pet a dog, and since guide dogs go to places where dogs usually cannot go, they get lots of attention. But we are reminded of the need for guide dogs not to be distracted while they are working, and it is our responsibility to educate our friends, family, co-workers, and even the people we meet to never touch or interact with your dog.

The second night, they gave us our leashes. This is the beginning of a ritual at The Seeing Eye, and I could not wait for the next part—when we clipped it on our dogs. Sue had already hinted about a dog for me. When we walked around the second day, she told me, "I have the perfect dog for you. You two have the same temperament. He's the most athletic dog in the group." But then she added something that made me laugh: "He also is the most beautiful dog I have ever trained. And he's going to be such a chick magnet."

I asked what kind of dog he was, and Sue said, "A Golden Retriever." I laughed at the irony.

I woke up day three as excited as Christmas morning. This was the day we meet our dogs, but we had to wait until after lunch. As soon as we ate, they told us to go to our rooms and wait until our instructors bring us our dog.

My room was at the end of the hall. My excitement had turned to anxiety, mixed with excitement. Since I am at the end of the hall, I heard nails on the floor, rattling of leashes, and other students squealing as their dogs enter their rooms. And I waited. And I waited. Clickity click after clickity click. Squeal after squeal.

I was pretty sure the next dog is mine. I heard nails. I heard panting, and I jumped off the bed. I opened my door. Sue said, "Here we come. You might want to sit." Like a well-trained dog, I recoiled back to my bed, and I sat. Sue brought him over to me, and I touched his head. His big, fluffy head. "His name is Tyrone," Sue said to me. "He is two years old, and he walks very, very fast." Tyrone is sitting in front of me, and I am petting him. He's nonchalant.

Then came the second part of The Seeing Eye ritual: Sue told me to take my leash and clip it on his collar. With hands slightly trembling, I opened the clip on the leash and snapped it in place. Within two seconds, Sue removed her leash. "He's your dog now."

Whoa. This was my dog. Sue left us, telling me she had to bring more dogs to people. "Get to know him," she said. "I'll give you an hour, and then we'll start working."

And she was gone. Man. What a mixture of emotions. I was seventeen years old, but in some ways, I felt like I was five because I was unsure of what to do. In some ways, though, I felt like I was thirty because I now have this super smart dog who would allow me to do so many things, and I would take care of him. And he would take care of me. So, I kept petting him. And then I talked to him. "Hey, Tyrone. How are you doing, buddy?" Stuff like that. He sat down. He leaned against me, and I kept running my hand down his long, strong back. It was so soft I could have curled up in it. After a while, I made his leash longer, and I couldn't wait another second. I stood up, and I walked around the room with him.

From those first steps, it was great.

Sue came back with a trial harness. I put it on him, and Sue connected a long cord to him. The three of us walked to the garden, Sue walking behind Tyrone and me. Tyrone evidently rotated between looking back at Sue and up at me. Sue told me to give him the motion for left and right. We turned left and turning right. And it is so smooth.

Tyrone eventually stopped looking at Sue, and he started looking at me. I signaled right. I signaled left. We were learning. And from the second we started, I liked it way more than a cane. You see, I was a bad blind person. I didn't use my cane. It was faster and easier to use someone's arm. When you are running with your buddies on the wrestling team, you learn to run and follow someone's footsteps. A cane is impossible to use when you were running. I had it with me, but I didn't use it. I mastered cane skills with Mrs. Michelson, but that was mainly to get me to this point.

I still had more learning to do. The first couple of days, Tyrone, Sue, and I walked mile after mile after mile. Even when we were not walking, Tyrone didn't leave my side. The only time we were apart was when I was in the shower. He became an extension of my left arm.

A Guide, a Companion, but Not a Pet

Dogs are not born with a fear of moving cars. Dogs cannot read street signs. Dogs cannot see the flashing white person icon in a crosswalk. Dogs do not know how to find the men's room in a mall. And all the breeding and training in the world cannot change that.

As intelligent as they are, guide dogs only know to do what their blind owners tell them to do. They turn right when we tell or signal them to turn right. They walk across the street when we tell them to walk across the street. Blind owners have to know where they are going and when they should go to tell the dogs. They are our eyes, but not our brains.

Tyrone being my eyes and not my pet was a distinction I made from the start. Yes, when I took his harness off and threw him a ball, he was a pet. And I loved that fluffy ball of fur. I cleaned his ears constantly because he is prone to ear infections. I brushed him every day. I brushed his teeth. I fed him morning and night. I picked up his natural byproduct. I bathed him every month. I wanted him around me all the time. But he was not a pet. We were a team. And becoming a team takes time.

Our first test was when Sue took us to a parking garage with lots of poles. She put the dogs and owners on one side of the poles and waited for us on the other side of the garage. She talked to us so that we could follow her voice. Her instructions were for us to get our dogs to her and see if they could maneuver us around the poles. I gave the commands. Tyrone followed them. He veered left and then right so that I wouldn't hit the poles. I was chuckling, realizing that I wouldn't have to go to the emergency room anymore with a bleeding forehead. Tyrone communicated something just by the way he pulled the leash. The pull told me how to move. It protected me. It increased my maneuverability. And I felt my confidence in him—in us—soar.

The Seeing Eye took us to a downtown area, and as we tried to cross a street, they sped a van around the corner to demonstrate that the dog is trained to employ "intelligent disobedience." Even if we have told the dog "forward," once the van appears, they must disobey. If they don't, they are corrected. I have to pull on his choke collar fast and hard. These corrections do not harm the dog. The choke collar mimics the action of a mother dog's nip on the back of her puppy's neck. It tells the dog on an instinctual level that they have done something they should not.

Before we left The Seeing Eye, Sue took us to New York City, just a short train ride from the campus. Here, all my mobility training paid off. I had to listen to the sound of the cars and tell Tyrone when to cross. Sue was with us, but she only intervened if there was a problem.

Amazingly, I found New York City very easy to navigate with Tyrone, and getting around the crowds was smooth. That's the best word I can use to describe it. Using a cane was jerky. Tyrone was smooth.

At the end of our training at The Seeing Eye, we got on a plane together, Tyrone and me. Tyrone tucked himself under the seat in front of me, and we were off for Florida for my senior year and the college adventure.

One of the Family

My Dad came to visit me at The Seeing Eye after I got Tyrone. He told me how gorgeous Tyrone was. I think his exact words, which he said over and over, were: "Kyle, that's a good-looking dog." And even though my dad loved Tyrone from the moment he saw him, he treated him differently than he treated Genevieve. Everyone in my family knew it had to be that way.

The first two days after I got home, my sisters couldn't talk to Tyrone or pet him. But after two days, The Seeing Eye told me I could take off his harness and leash, and they could pet him.

As easy a transition as it was into increased mobility with Tyrone, each day, each week, each month, it got better and smoother. I can't tell you that he was the best guide dog ever, but he was better than most people. His lack of perfection is exactly what I needed—and any blind person needs—to keep the partnership in balance.

Here's an example. At my high school graduation, Tyrone walked across the stage with me as I got my diploma. (The senior class voted "Joined at the Hip.") I was the only blind student at my school, and Tyrone was the only dog on stage that day, so there were some cheers and murmurs as we appeared. Maybe Tyrone got a little spooked, but he stopped before the stairs down from the platform. The audience thought we would jump off the risers, and there was a bit of a collective gasp. Luckily, Mrs. Michelson, my O&M instructor, was at the bottom of the stairs, and she called to me. Hearing her voice, I directed Tyrone "forward," and we made it off without mishap. I was never in danger, and I thought it was funny. The audience made a worst-case assumption in a split second, but it was a reminder that I always have to be in charge of my safety.

If there was a moment when I felt like Tyrone and I gelled as a team, I would pick Mother's Day 2010. He had been my seeing-eye dog for eleven months. For my mom's special day, she wanted to pack a picnic lunch and go to a park on Fernandina Beach. Genevieve came, and of course, Tyrone was there. John came, too, as he is basically a member of the family. After we ate, Mom wanted to take a walk — through trails to the ocean.

We cleaned up our lunch and took off. I was in the lead, and Tyrone was walking step for step. Genevieve and my baby sister, Caitlin, were in the rear with my Mom. Cassandra and Kelsey were in the middle of the family pack. Dad and John were with me, and Dad tells me up ahead is a sand dune and us four men should take it. "It's on the right," Dad says. Just as I was about to give Tyrone the command, he smelled the ocean. And he took off. He was running and dragging me with my feet kicking up sand behind me. Tyrone was seriously hauling.

Over the sound of the waves, I heard my mom and Caitlin laughing, and they were jogging with Genevieve to catch up. Suddenly, we were all there, at the water's edge, laughing and saying, "What the heck got into Tyrone?" My only answer was, "My dog is possessed." My Mom summed it all up perfectly when she said, "Go figure that mountain boy gets a beach dog."

Beach or mountain, a big city or home, Tyrone was my guide. With his incredible speed when we walked together, I found that feeling again, with arms outstretched, flying over an enchanted island, safe from harm. And I knew that no matter how high the peak I summit, Tyrone was waiting for me when I came down.

To learn more about The Seeing Eye or make a donation toward its important work for the blind, please visit www.seeingeye.org. The Seeing Eye receives no government funds and relies solely on the contributions from individuals, corporations, and foundations.

Chapter 14

The Beginning of Team Sight Unseen

A Dream

Sitting in a tent at 14,300 feet on the Super Inca Trail, Justin turned to me and said, "K Coon, what do you think about doing Denali?"

"I think it'd be awesome but a little outside our range right now."

A year later, we stood atop Mt. Kilimanjaro. And on the way down from Kibo to Horombo Hut, Justin and I began to talk. We both wanted to keep climbing, and we wanted to keep climbing with the other members of our team. Now that we had one of the Seven Summits under our belts, we were eager to go after more. Justin kept talking about wanting to do Denali — Mt. McKinley, the tallest mountain in North America. I thought it was a little more sensible to try something a little less technical than the 20,320-foot behemoth of Alaska. Maybe we could try something like Mt. Elbrus — the tallest peak in Europe.

One thing was certain; we couldn't climb without a team. Over the past two years, we'd listened to Erik, Eric, Jeff, and Didrik and read books on mountaineering. While there were many great mountaineers, those who seemed to be the most fulfilled were those with strong teams. Erik and Eric had both told us on numerous occasions that their Everest team probably didn't have all world-class climbers. But each climber on the team had a role and played it perfectly.

People often try to say that teams are like well-oiled machines. If one part screws up or is dysfunctional, it will throw off the whole machine and cause it to break down. Others like to say that the team is only as strong as its weakest link. If it fails, then the chain breaks, and therefore the team fails. Or even like a wheel, if one or more spokes break, the wheel bends and doesn't work correctly.

Climbing teams are not this way. Climbing teams are living, breathing organisms. When a person is healthy, and their body is getting the right amounts of oxygen, food, water, and such and is in a stable state, it's called homeostasis. In this state, the body is the well-oiled machine, unbroken chain, or the wheel with all its spokes. The difference between a human body and those other objects is that everything's not lost if there's a bump in the road.

Let's say the person gets sick. All those cells that were minding their own business don't stop and point the finger at the immune system and say, "You weren't doing your job." No. They lend their support and combined energies to reaching that homeostatic state once more. The body heals while still pushing onward and upward. A mountaineering team is no different.

Justin and I wanted to build a team around us with bonds of friendship, skill, and drive. We wanted the strongest team. And we had the foundation of that from our group of Global Explorers teammates.

Over the next few weeks and months following our ascent of Kilimanjaro, we talked to everyone from our Kili team. Only Brad seemed sincerely interested in pushing the boundaries a little further with us. Everyone else was starting to go their separate ways.

Peru and Kilimanjaro had been great life-changing adventures, but people were starting to look toward their careers, college, and life in general. Hiking and climbing were recreational to most. So, Brad, Justin, and I came together.

We had no idea where to start or what to do. We knew we wanted to climb mountains together. And we knew that we needed a strong team. But how did we go about building that team that we envisioned? How did we assemble that living, breathing organism with the ability to improvise, adapt and overcome the obstacles?

We emailed and talked on the phone almost nightly. We had email and phone conversations with Eric Alexander, Erik Weihenmayer, and Jeff Evans. We badgered them with questions on finding team members, fundraising for climbs, and what climbs to do. We were sure about one thing, and that was that we needed to identify ourselves as a team. We needed a brand, an identity: we needed a name.

Brad, Justin, and I had some in-depth philosophical discussions about what the mountains did for each of us. For all of us, there was a consistent theme of "The journey," or "The summit just wasn't the best part," or "The destination just wouldn't have meant as much if we didn't have to work to get there."

"I'd recently read a book, and a wise, old character named Ramón advised, "When you can have anything you want by uttering a few words, the goal matters not, only the journey to it." What I took away from that was, "It's not the destination, but the journey that makes the trip worthwhile." What name could we give ourselves that would embody that ideal of the journey and spoke to what we were—a group of blind and sighted climbers?

Finally, we came up with the name "Sight Unseen." It seemed to fit us, our ideas about climbing, and our outlooks on life as well.

Building The Team

Shortly after returning from Africa, I decided that I'd try my hand at writing. I'd written a couple of dispatches that we sent over the Web while in Tanzania. And my teachers had always complimented me on my essays and storytelling ability. So I decided to try and tell my story to a larger audience.

I wrote a short piece about our climb of Kilimanjaro and submitted it to "Backpacker Magazine." They published the piece in the Winter 2007 issue. It didn't take long for the story to impact someone.

Nearly 3,000 miles away, in Eugene, Oregon, Peter Green picked up his copy of Backpacker Magazine and read the 400-word reader submission entitled "The Mt. Kilimanjaro Expedition." And in February 2008, Global Explorers forwarded me an email from Peter Green.

Peter was an avid climber and had a mother and sister who were legally blind. He'd found the story I'd written very inspirational and was wondering if I'd ever considered hiking the Pacific Crest Trail. The PCT is a hiking trail that stretches from Mexico to Canada. It's the west coast version of the Appalachian Trail. If I was interested, Peter volunteered to help me achieve that goal.

Curious to find out more about this guy, I responded to his email expressing a possible interest in his idea but requested more information about his personal climbing experience, job, family, and choosing to contact me. He replied and gave me his climbing credentials and history.

Having grown up in the Pacific Northwest, Peter got involved with Boy Scouts and then rock climbing and backpacking. He eventually progressed to overall mountaineering and climbed most of the Cascade Volcanoes, made several snowboard descents of Mt. St. Helens, and completed several other challenging climbs around the Pacific Northwest. In addition, he was a member of the Eugene, Oregon Mountain Search and Rescue and was a Wilderness First Responder.

Eventually, emails led to phone conversations. And then Peter became a resource. He was willing and able to teach Brad, Justin, and me what we needed to learn about the mountains. And in July 2008, Brad and I flew out to Oregon to partake in a mini mountaineering class that Peter designed to teach us the technical side of mountaineering.

We were familiar with Leave No Trace and first aid, but neither of us knew about self-arrest, crevasse rescue, or glacier travel, and we'd need to know how to do these and more if we wanted to continue our climbing careers. Peter taught us.

Sitting on the side of Mt. Hood, Brad and I tied all different types of knots in climbing rope: figure-eight, figure-eights on a bite, butterfly, double and triple fishermans, and clove and Munter hitches were just a few.

We hiked up a steep snowy slope, then slid down on our butts, rolled over onto our fronts, and plunged the pick of an ice-axe into the snow to stop our slide. We practiced stopping ourselves from sliding downhill from all different positions. We'd lay on our backs with our head pointing downhill and then have to flip over and stop using our axe. We practiced slipping, falling, and arresting. We learned how to build snow anchors to belay each other up or down a steep snow slope.

We filled a backpack up with snow and threw it over a cliff attached to a rope to practice hauling up an injured person out of a crevasse. We rigged up a system on a ski lift tower to practice getting ourselves out of a crevasse by sliding prusik knots up the rope.

There was never a dull moment or downtime. I'd known that true mountaineering was a lot of work and took mind and willpower, but never had my brain been flooded with so much information on what, when, how, and why to do things in the mountains.

After two days of learning mountaineering techniques, Peter, Brad, and I hiked up to 9,000 feet on Mt. Hood. We pitched our tents at a spot called Illumination Saddle. The snow, rock, and ice conditions higher up the mountain weren't ideal for a summit attempt at that point in the season. We planned to camp then head down in the morning.

From the side of Hood, we watched the fiery reds, oranges, and yellows as the sun stained the clouds all types of brilliant hues. We breathed of the crisp snowy air. The wind began to rise. And we marveled at the beauty of the mountains.

Mt. St. Helens

I'd once read a poem in middle school that was an example of an extended metaphor. The poem spoke of a monstrous goddess who showed no mercy to those around her and whose beauty was unmatched. She was both a queen and monstrous despite her stature. The metaphor was referring to Mt. St. Helens.

When I'd read that poem in middle school, I didn't know that I'd one day attempt to reach the 8,500-foot summit of St. Helens. But that's what Brad, Pete, and I were going to try next. The only trouble: we didn't have permits.

We tried to talk with the person in charge of issuing permits, but no success. We settled for climbing up to about 4,200 feet and camp. Since we were allowed to be below 4,800 feet without a permit, we parked at the trailhead and loaded up our packs, and set off up the trail.

It started smooth, but soon we started rock hopping. We clambered up, over and around giant lava rocks. Before long, it was time to pull over and pitch our tents. For fun, we even built a snow shelter by digging into the side of the mountain. And we just relaxed all afternoon. And the more we sat on the side of the mountain, the more we yearned to stand on top. We decided that, rather than going down, we'd go for the summit in the morning.

We awoke at 5:30 a.m. and left camp at 6 a.m. Peter had climbed and snowboarded Mt. St. Helens a couple of months earlier and figured we were about a three to four-hour climb from the summit. But as soon as we stepped out onto the trail, I had a hard time. I was using my hands just as much as my feet to pull myself up on top of rocks, balanced precariously next to deep gashes between rocks, and avoided slipping and tumbling down snow slopes. Eventually, we reached a long snow slope, and we began kicking our boots into the slope.

I leaned on my ice-axe, breathing heavily. I felt my heels blistering in the rented mountaineering boots I wore. I could hear the bells dangling from Brad's back, up ahead of me. I sucked at the thinning air as we climbed higher and higher. There were times when I just sank to my knees and used a technique known as low daggering to stab the pick of my axe into the snow to help pull me up the steep snow slope.

What Peter thought would take us four hours took us nearly six. We made the last push up a steep scree field to the summit. Then we raised our axes to the sky and cheered. I was cheerful that the hard part was over. Boy, was I wrong.

The Summit's only the halfway point.

We spent 15 minutes on the summit and then turned around and started heading back the way we'd come. Brad wanted to try his hand at glissading so that we could practice our self-arrest techniques more. We began scouting for snow patches to practice. We found several and began sliding downhill, rolling over and plunging our axes into the snow if we needed to stop. Then we ran out of snow. And when Pete and Brad looked around, they noticed that we were well off the main descent path far off to our left. We had to traverse across and down to get back on track. Okay, no big deal.

Brad took the lead, and we began down, climbing and traversing across the mountain. Then we hit massive piles of lava rocks. These jagged, roughly hewn boulders were responsible for more than a few gashes, scrapes, and cuts that ran from my ankles to thighs and down both arms.

We picked our way through and across the boulders, but they only kept getting bigger, and the mountainside kept getting steeper. Finally, we could see the trail, but we needed to cross a snowfield pitched at about sixty degrees to reach it. No big deal except that only about sixty feet below was the largest jumble of lava rocks we'd seen. On a snow slope higher up, one of my trekking poles had snapped cleanly in two when I'd needed to catch myself to keep from falling face-first downhill.

I had my ice-axe to my pack and had one trekking pole to use. Pete gave me one of his and then inched his way across the snowfield. All the while looking down between his feet at the treacherous end he'd come to if he fell. Then Brad inched his way across. Next was my turn.

I pressed my chest and hips into the snow and firmly kicked in my boots. Next, I reached out with my right pole and stabbed as deep into the slope as I could. Then my left pole. My right foot moved right and kicked in, followed by my left. At all times, I had three points of contact with the snow slope, in addition to my torso, which I tried to keep pressed into the slope as often as I could.

Watching me, Pete chuckled, "Kyle, don't worry, if you fall, you'll only hit a pile of rocks and cartwheel five or six times before hitting your head on a rock and snapping your neck." (Thanks, Pete. Real encouraging.)

I safely made it across.

After that, it was just a crazy scramble over rocks back to the trail. Then down the trail to camp, where we broke down our tents, packed up, and headed downhill.

Three hours after this, we stumbled into the parking lot caked from head to toe in volcanic ash, dust, and general filth. Add in a few scrapes, bruises, and quarter-sized blisters on my heels; we were a little worse for wear. We'd been in our boots for 12 hours. We'd started hiking at 6 a.m. and reached the car at 6 p.m. We were ready to fill our bellies with something hot, greasy, and satisfying. We stopped and ate burgers, pizza, and wings washing it all down with several sodas on the drive back to Oregon.

We had one more day with Pete before he had to drop us off at the airport in Portland and decided to take a break from climbing to have a little fun at the Mt. Hood Ski Bowl—a mini amusement park. We spent the day bungee jumping and sliding down the "alpine slide." The alpine slide was essentially a bobsled run, and we sat on wheeled carts that we could make go faster by pushing a little handle forward.

Brad took off down the run, trying to make it down as fast as he possible in hopes of catching a video of Pete and me. I opened my cart full throttle as Pete slid behind, yelling when to turn. Slightly more than three-quarters of the way down, he accidentally called out a wrong turn, and I went head over heels, sliding across a slight scree slope as my cart pinwheeled behind me. Don't feel sorry for me. I was laughing the whole way hysterically—as was Brad. Brad had managed to get onto a small bridge overlooking the slide and was just about to take the video when I wiped out. I came out of it with just a few extra scrapes.

We spent our last night swimming in the lake at our campsite. We floated, treaded water, and talked about what the future held for us as climbers. The three of us had bonded so quickly, and Brad and I both felt we could trust Pete with our lives in the mountains. After returning home and discussing it over the phone with Justin, we extended an invitation to Pete to join Team Sight Unseen. He accepted, bringing us one step closer. Justin brought on his climbing partner Joseph Mayfield, and Pete recruited one of his climbing partners, Ben Meyer. And with that, we had a team of six. Now we needed a mountain to climb.

Chapter 15

Success! Without a Summit?

August 18, 2010. Gannett Peak, Wyoming. Elevation, about 10,200 ft

I was tightly packed in my sleeping bag thinking about the day ahead when I heard Brad and Ben begin to move around and talk in the tent just a few feet from the one that Joe, Justin, and I were sharing, and I knew that the time had come.

Brad came over and shook the poles of our tent, calling out, "Time to get up, boys." I immediately sat up and unzipped myself from my very warm sleeping bag.

I had worn my summit clothes and bibs to sleep in preparation for today, and I had pretty much packed what I needed just a few hours before. It was 1 a.m. and cold. I fumbled with numb fingers as I undid the Ziploc bag that held my supply of gauze pads and medical tape. Then I proceeded to wrap my heels to attempt to prevent the already quarter-size blisters on the backs of my heels from getting any larger. Then I pulled on thick hiking socks and shoved my feet into my La Sportivas that I had been continuing to break-in at the start of this trip. I finished dressing, unzipped the tent, and crawled out, ready for the day.

I went over to our cook tent for breakfast, hot drinks, and to discuss the day's strategy. I was shivering as I sipped hot chocolate, and I thought about the day ahead. I couldn't deny that I was nervous. The boulder field that we'd partially climbed through and made our camp next to was a blind person's worst nightmare, with no patterns in the jumbled boulders whatsoever. Throughout this trip, I'd grown a much greater appreciation for what kinds of things my friend and mentor, Erik Weihenmayer, had climbed and the mental exhaustion he often talked about getting in the mountains.

But before I could overthink that, it was time to head out. I strapped my backpack, which contained nothing but my ice-axe, crampons, a proshell jacket Ben had lent me after telling me my particular heavy/rain jacket wasn't fit for climbing, two liters of water, and a few snacks for the entire day. I was wearing all the layers that I thought I'd need for the day's climb. I picked up my trekking poles and then set out, following Brad through the boulder field on our way up towards the summit.

Brad stepped from boulder to boulder ringing the bells we'd brought to help me follow him easier. He also directed me where to place each of my feet. "Left foot to a big flat rock. Right foot match. Reach out with your trekking pole to this rock I'm on. Try to fit your right foot up here. Careful. It's wobbly. Now do a dynamic move and bring your left foot forward and up between these two rocks to a flat spot." More times than not, Brad would take my poles in his hands and place them where he wanted me to step. It was an endless game of what we called "Boulder Hopping."

Brad, Justin, Ben, and I climbed for two straight hours through the boulder field before taking our first break. At that point, Peter and Joe (who'd both started an hour after us) caught up with us, and we continued picking our way up the boulder field for another couple of hours. Finally, we reached snow only to find that it was a brief relief, for we crossed over to another boulder field and climbed up this one. Then came the same rain/hail combination that had forced Ben, Joe, and me to hunker down in a small rock cave two days earlier when we'd first reached the boulder field and prevented us from reaching what we hoped would be our high camp. Fortunately, this storm blew over quickly, but unfortunately, it didn't take the pain in my right heel away with it.

Since the beginning of the trip, I'd had some pretty severe blisters and had been regularly taping and re-taping them to prevent as much rubbing as possible. Now, after hours and hours of boulder hopping, I was finally starting to notice the pain. We finally climbed off the boulder field and began working up a steep snow slope to take us to another boulder field. From there, we would continue onto the snow slope that would lead us to the bergschrund and then finally to the summit. With every step I kicked into the snow, the pain in my heel worsened. "Ignore it. It's all in your head. You're fine," I kept telling myself. But at the same time, the pain grew, and I remembered all the things I knew about mountaineering. Peter's three goals of every trip were "Safety, fun, summit," and I'd adopted them as my three goals for trips. Then I remembered the long way we'd come and that we still had to hike that whole way back to the cars at the trailhead, almost 25 miles or so from where we were now.

By this time, we'd climbed up to about 11,600 feet, still 2200 feet below the summit. From my ankles to my neck, I felt in as great a shape as I ever had been. But my heel was becoming more unbearably painful with every step I took. I knew what I had to do.

I told Joe (who'd taken over guiding me partway up the boulder field to give Brad a break) that my heel was really hurting, and I needed to stop for a while. Peter encouraged me to climb up to the next boulder field, where we'd have a team talk about how everyone was doing. So, we did. And when I sat down to rest, I pulled off my boot and sock and ripped off the tape covering my blister. I felt my heel. It wasn't the blister that was bothering me, and as my fingers explored further, I found where I was hurting. The base of my Achilles tendon that attached to my heel was swollen and sent jolts of pain up my leg every time I moved my foot in any direction. I tried massaging it a little, but the pain didn't go away. Peter asked me how I was doing, and I told him not well at all. Then we began to talk about all the possibilities. If I were to go down, who would accompany me, who would go to the summit, or would everybody turn around. I knew that everyone else was feeling strong and wanted to go on to the summit.

I thought about how my heel felt, how the rest of my body felt, and the long climb to the summit while thinking about the long climb down to high camp and the hike down past high camp and back to the trailhead. I knew that I would go down now rather than risk my swollen Achilles worsening by pushing on.

Trying to hold back tears, I told the team that I didn't think that there was any way I could safely climb to the summit and then hike back down with the way my ankle and heel were feeling. Then to my surprise, Justin piped up and said that if I wasn't going to summit, he didn't want to either. His philosophy was in the "all for one and one for all" way of thinking. "We summit as a team, and we don't summit as a team," he might have been saying.

I knew that everyone else was disappointed because Peter had laid out the circumstances to us the night before. If I turned around, then Brad would accompany me back to high camp. If Justin turned around, then Joe would accompany him back to high camp. And if both of us turned around, then the whole team would turn around. I knew that by choosing to turn around, I would cost Peter, Ben, Brad, and Joe a chance at the summit and the chance of gaining more mountaineering experience. When we decided to turn around, I had an enormous feeling of guilt and sadness in my heart. Ben, Peter, Brad, and Joe all climbed up to the top of a rock to take one last longing look at the summit. Once they got up there, they saw that the path wasn't more than a two-and-a-half-hour journey from where we currently were. They returned to where Justin and I were sitting, readying ourselves to go down, and explained to us what they had seen and thought of, making it clear that if we disapproved of their plan, then we'd go straight down with no hesitation.

The plan was for Peter, Ben, Brad, and Joe to go unroped, carry as little gear as possible and a little water, and to go for a speed ascent up the next couple of snow and rock pitches to the top, quickly summit, then come down, grab Justin and me and head down to high camp. Granted, that would mean Justin and I would wait for several hours while the rest of the guys were climbing, but I knew that they all wanted the summit, and I knew that they all deserved to summit. I immediately agreed to the plan, and so did Justin. The guys left their remaining gear with us and began their speed ascent towards the top.

After an hour or more of their being gone, Justin and I rigged up a small sun shelter using rocks, a couple of foam sleeping pads, and our backpacks. While we rigged this shelter up and sat in it for several hours, we talked and thought a lot about the trip. I asked myself what

I was getting out of this trip and whether I could still consider our climb a success even though I hadn't summitted.

Day 1: Trailhead to Downs Fork Meadows

Moving out on Day 1. Brad (middle) leads Kyle (back) with Ben leading the way for everyone.

We arrived at the trailhead late on the night of August 13, 2010, and quickly set up our camp. We were a mixed group, three from Oregon (Pete, Monica, and Ben), two from Texas (Justin and Joe), one from Wisconsin (Brad), and me, the Florida flatlander. We were Team Sight Unseen, and we had won a $10,000 grant from W.L Gore and Associates to help pay for this trip, which we were using as a training climb for a future trip to Aconcagua.

We got to bed somewhere around midnight and woke up around 5 or 5:30 a.m. to sort and pack our gear into our backpacks, which the horse packers would be taking for the first couple of days. Peter held what we called TSU Christmas, where he handed out all the gear we had purchased with the grant from GORE-TEX. I received a pair of La Sportiva mountaineering boots (which I had received two months earlier and started breaking in), an ice ax, and new pair of gloves. The others received things like helmets, gaiters, knives, and several other small items. As group gear, we'd purchased a couple of new MSR tents, and GORE-TEX had made us performance T-Shirts with the Team Sight Unseen and GORE-TEX logos on them.

It finally came time to load up the horses and get moving. Pete and Monica stayed behind to help the horse packers load the horses while Ben, Brad, Justin, Joe, and I got going on the trail. We had 16 miles to travel, and it was going to take most of the day. Brad and Ben each carried a daypack with a supply of water. Brad, Justin, and I would pass Brad's pack among the three of us, so each of us carried the pack for at least a few hours throughout the day. We took about a break every hour to an hour and a half and hiked about two miles per hour. The terrain was rolling, sometimes going up and other times going down, sometimes quite flat. For that first half of the day, we mostly went uphill. We reached the high point of that first day (about 10,800 feet) between noon and 1 o'clock, just about four hours after we started hiking and which was about the halfway point, so we figured that we'd take a longer break in a little while and then we'd probably reach camp between 4 and 5 o'clock.

We cruised down through flat down-sloping meadows before hitting some rocky boulder fields. I usually enjoy boulder fields if they are early in the day because they provide a mind game, forcing me to concentrate on every step. However, this trip would teach me to hate boulder fields. And this first boulder field was minuscule compared to those we would encounter higher up. We took our break around 3:00 and then pushed on at about 3:45 in the afternoon. We'd already come at least ten, and I was already weary and more than a little footsore. I knew that I just had to keep pushing onward, and eventually, we'd get to camp.

I kept pushing, and we kept climbing, then descending, then climbing again. We climbed down what seemed an endless series of switchbacks down to one of several lakes. Then we climbed down even more switchbacks and even more. I was both physically and mentally exhausted when I stumbled into camp around 7:30 that evening. I had massive blisters on my heels, and all I wanted to do was collapse in my sleeping bag and fall asleep.

That night we had a relatively good dinner of lamb tips with assorted vegetables. I soaked my feet in the glacial streams that covered the mountain. And although my feet shrieked in agony at contact with the icy water, it was quite soothing. Finally, we crawled into our sleeping bags and fell asleep.

Day 2: Downs Fork Meadows to Gannett Creek

I woke up sore but able to move. My blisters hurt, but I knew I could prevent an overwhelming amount of rubbing with a little gauze and tape. The previous night I staggered into camp, hardly able to stand after the last miles dragged on for what seemed like forever. I had thought that I wouldn't be able to get up or even move, but the restorative powers of sleep do a man wonders.

I arose, doctored my heels, ate breakfast, and prepared to depart camp. Brad guided me again, and we made decent time. While on the first part of the trail, the whole team stuck together, and we began discussing some in-depth plans and ideas for the future. Today was supposed to only be about six (although we all agreed later that we thought the distance was mismarked) with minimal elevation gain. We did, however, pass through some magnificent scenery. We hiked along a beach made by glacier deposits alongside a glacier-fed lake. We saw intense rapids and before long caught the first sight of our objective, Wyoming's high point: Gannett Peak.

We stood upon a rocky shelf and gazed toward our goal, and I felt that thrill that always seemed to possess me when I am in the mountains and when we first caught sight of our goal. Many climbers feel this pull, the attraction of a summit like an irresistible magnetic pull, or possibly even a gravitational one. Climbers are often caught in the orbits of summits even when we are far away from them. Take me, for instance, I lived in Florida, but for some reason, despite the pain of gigantic blisters, the soreness, the weather, the heartbreak of not reaching the top, I continue to be drawn back.

The team and the first view of Gannett Peak. (L-R): Justin, Joe, Peter, Kyle, Brad, Ben.

We continued crossing over several small streams, wet and dry beds, and before long came upon a rather tiring boulder field. This boulder field was slightly larger than the one we had come through just after the high point of the previous day, and therefore we took it slower. The rocks were slightly larger. A few were looser and, on the whole, more of a head and foot ache. Finally, though, we came out of it and reached camp between 3:30 and 4 o'clock.

After setting up camp, I removed my boots and let my feet air out before walking down to the creek and soaking my feet in icy water again. Then returning to the tents, I proceeded to attempt to inflate my Thermarest. I had discovered on the first night I had used the Thermarest that there was a hole in one of the corners. Joe and I doctored the hole with tape, and I proceeded to inflate it. But the air I was blowing into it concentrated at the damaged corner, and slowly the adhesive that held the foam inside of the Thermarest began to peel away from the inside. Brad videotaped my attempts to blow the pad up, and we all laughed considerably harder as the pad bore more and more the resemblance of a hotdog. I soon gave up, deflated the little bit that I had inflated, and just lay down on the pad on the grass outside the tent and commenced the relaxation part of the day before a dinner of tuna fish tacos, rice, and beans. I typically don't like fish, but my taste buds seem to leave me, and I just eat to get the calories when I'm in the mountains.

After dinner, we discussed the principles of "Leave No Trace" and discussed how best we could practice LNT and how we could educate and influence others to do the same. We all felt strongly that these beautiful places we explored and hiked through deserved to be preserved.

Day 3: The Climbing Begins

This day would be the first day that we'd climb while carrying our packs. We attempted to distribute the gear evenly. Each of us carried at least 50 pounds of personal and team gear. Justin's pack and my pack were the lightest (weighing about 50 pounds each), while Brad, Joe, and Ben each carried about 65 to 70 pounds, and Peter carried the most (probably anywhere from 80 to 90 pounds).

Ben and Joe set out first to reach Gannett Creek, which was apparently a very wide and rough crossing. They intended to set up a rope across for everyone to use as a hand line. Brad, Justin, and I set out soon after them. The going was relatively easy until we reached the creek.

Gannett Creek was indeed a wide and slightly unnerving crossing. (Not really what you think of when you hear "creek"). The crossing consisted of two logs leading from the bank to a small island halfway across the creek and then another log leading from this island to the far bank. Once across, Joe guided me a short way over a series of creeks and up to a point where the ground began to rise sharply up toward a meadow.

Justin (left) and Kyle (right) resting at the Gannett Creek crossing.

Brad and Justin joined us, and Brad took over the guiding while Joe went back to help Ben break down the hand line. Brad, Justin, and I climbed upwards, slowly and deliberately, stopping every little bit for water. We eventually started walking slightly uphill through a meadow toward a large series of rocks. Ben and Joe caught up with us, and we all continued until almost lunchtime. We then sat to wait for Pete and Monica.

Several of us fell asleep in the nice weather on the sun-warmed rocks. After lunch with Pete and Monica, Ben took over, guiding me with Joe backseat driving, and everyone else surged on ahead to try to get to and set up camp. We were confident that we'd make good time to camp and have plenty of time to rest and relax before dinner. But we ran into a blind guy's worse nightmare: a boulder field.

I'd encountered boulder fields before, but none like this one. I was just as often using my hands as my feet to climb up, around, and between boulders. Ben and Joe directed me as best they could, "left pole out to this rock where I'm standing. Right pole match and bring right foot between your poles. Now give me your poles and use the rock on your right as a handrail and come up between these rocks and then up and over the ones on the other side." And it continued for what seemed like forever.

Then the rain and hail came. We dug our rain gear out and continued while the hail pelted us, and the wind whipped around, making it more challenging to hear Ben's directions. Ben and Joe constantly looked around for a possible shelter and finally found one under an overhanging rock. We scrambled over to it and hunkered down, waiting for the weather to pass over. Ben began trying to contact Pete on the radio, and Joe introduced a guessing game to pass the time. We could ask yes or no questions about what animal Joe was thinking, and we eventually guessed the animal. Although a ridiculous game in general, it was a great way to pass the time while sheltering beneath a rock in a mini-storm.

We finally contacted Brad via radio. He told us that Pete was on his way down to find us and communicated that our intended camp was flooded (under about 5 to 6 feet of water). When Pete reached us, we discussed the possibilities of camping either up further or closer to where we were. There was a snowfield right beside where we were hunkering down. Ben, Joe, and I began cutting tent platforms while Pete climbed back up through the boulders to reach Brad, Justin, and Monica. Eventually, we were all ensconced at camp and preparing for a rest day the following day.

Day 4: A Much Needed Rest

We'd set aside the fourth day as a rest day to ensure we'd be at our peak for reaching the peak. Ben led us through a series of knot and self-arrest reviews. It was a great opportunity to feel the varying amounts of force a rope team could put on someone in self-arrest, and it was a lot harder to hold a rope team than I initially thought. It was also great to review all the knots and various anchors.

Pete and Monica then surprised us with an amazing backcountry pepperoni pizza, probably the best meal on the trail.

Brad then took us through a brief course about orienteering. Although I won't use much of this, it was still an interesting topic and refreshed what I knew about orienteering. We got to bed early in preparation for summit day.

Day 5: Summit-Down

The team happy at "our" high point.

As Justin and I waited in our improvised shelter, we talked and joked, laughing at our absolute brilliance of using foam ridge rests, trekking poles, backpacks, rocks, and jackets to rig up our sun shelter. We sat and talked about the climb thus far and the long climb down. And we talked through Justin's philosophy of "All for one and one for all." Neither of us felt exceptionally bad about the others going on to the summit without us. There was a little jealousy because now the others would have the bragging rights of another summit, but Justin and I both understood the importance of experience in the mountains, and we all felt that it would be highly beneficial for the rest of the crew to do a speed ascent up to the summit and then back down to collect us.

After a more than four-hour wait, we finally spotted Pete, Ben, Brad, and Joe. They climbed down to us, ecstatic at their success in reaching the summit. We congratulated them and felt happy that at least four of us got the chance to stand atop Gannett Peak.

We waited for the four summiteers to rest and replenish their strength through a few bites of Goldfish crackers and gummy bears before shouldering our packs and beginning the long trek down toward high camp.

It was long and arduous. I was constantly positioning and repositioning my feet on loose and slippery rocks. Fortunately, though, we were descending and could pick out better paths than we had on the way up. We walked on snow as often as we could before finally entering the last stretch of boulder fields before camp.

Monica greeted us at camp with ham and cheese on crackers and much-needed fluids. That night we had a dinner of cold pasta salad that Monica had prepared while we'd been up higher on the mountain. It was delicious after a long day of rock scrambling.

Day 6: High Camp to Horse Packers Camp

We got up early and began the descent, with Brad leading me through the boulder fields. Once we got out of the boulder field, Joe took over guiding and led me for a little more than an hour. (Brad, Ben, and Joe rotated, guiding me for an hour each for the remainder of the trip.) We descended as fast as we could through the meadow and then made it to the Gannett Creek crossing. Ben and Joe set up the handline again, and we got across and took a break for lunch.

After lunch, it seemed to take forever to reach Downs Fork Meadows. When Ben and I were cruising through the meadow and beach area beside the glacier lake, it seemed as though every 10 minutes, we thought we'd be getting out and be descending again, but we just kept on walking. We finally reached Downs Fork around 5 o'clock, and we were all beat. I was about middle of the road and wouldn't have argued if we decided to push on, but we were all exhausted and ready to collapse on the whole.

Pete built a fire and commenced making our dinner of tortilla soup. We passed around snack food and candy bars as we waited for the food to finish cooking. We talked again about his reasons we had all decided to stay here at camp even though it meant a 16-mile hike the next day and again the reasons why Pete, Ben, Brad, and Joe had chosen to go to the summit leaving Justin and me to wait at the rock outcrop.

Justin and I talked a bit about our eye conditions and the things we could all do as a team to improve our communication and climbing. Eventually, we retired for the night between 9 and 10 p.m. to be up and rolling out of camp by 2 a.m.

Day 7: To get to Heaven, You Have to Go Through Hell

Sixteen miles with fifty-to-eighty-pound backpacks was just asking for one of us to quit mountaineering. But it wasn't going to happen.

We got up a little after 1 a.m. and quickly packed our gear. We strapped on our packs and rolled out of camp just before 2 a.m. We had a long series of switchbacks to climb up, and we knew that this would take most of the morning, so we pushed on moving as fast as we dared without burning ourselves out. My blisters hurt, but the thought of the cars waiting at the trailhead and the promise of hot non-trail food that night was a great pain killer.

Justin was having a rough time, but we all encouraged him to keep pushing on. But of course, we later joked that male pride must have had a major effect on Justin's turning the gears up a notch and motoring on. Pete suggested, "Hey Justin, if your packs feeling a bit heavy, we packed Monica's pack a little lighter today, so she's free to take on a little more weight." After that, we all cranked out the miles before us like champs.

We hiked through a burned-out forested area. Climbed up steep rocky hillsides and finally reached a long uphill grassy slope that led to the highest point of the day about eight miles from the trailhead. Joe and I reached it just a few minutes behind Brad, Ben, and Justin. Pete and Monica followed us up about five or ten minutes later.

Ben took over, guiding me, and we tried our best to push forward fast downhill. After a couple more hours, I let my feet air out, and Pete took over, guiding me. Pete, Monica, and I had a leisurely stroll through a beautiful high alpine meadow before we met up with Brad and Justin some distance below. Ben and Joe had gotten inspired and cruised on ahead to reach the trailhead and the cars. They planned to be ready with water and snacks for us all when we came into the parking lot.

Brad, Justin, and I remembered our descent of Kilimanjaro three years earlier as we kicked it into our highest gear. We laughed at how similar this descent was to that of Kilimanjaro— everyone going all out to reach the bottom, to reach the promise of good food, drink, and rest. The summit may be one hell of a magnet or gravitational pull to resist, but home is an even harder one to resist.

Brad leads Kyle and Justin on the final day.

Brad, Justin, and I cruised downhill on endless switchbacks passing many climbers on their way up, whether for a day hike or a hope for the summit. We didn't honestly care. We just wanted to get down. The last hour of our trek seemed to take much longer through an almost alpine desert-like area. This last hour was made even harder by the fact that we'd run out of water. But finally, we came in sight of the trailhead, and there were Ben and Joe with water, cans of fruit juice, and big smiles. Joe lifted my hat and dumped a bottle of water on my head. The first shower I'd taken in a week, and man, it felt good.

That night in Jackson Hole, we sat around several tables that we'd pushed together in a barbecue restaurant. Before, on a snowboarding trip to Wyoming, Brad had been to this restaurant and swore it was the best barbecue in the world. He obviously has never had some serious BBQ in the south, but I'll give him a pass—for now.

We recapped our trip, chugged Pepsi, and stuffed our faces with pork, chicken, baked beans, and corn. Pete, Monica, Ben, and Brad all indulged in drinking Coronas (oh, how I wished I'd been 21). We all toasted a great trip and wondered when the next time we would all climb together would be. I was heading back to Florida for my second semester at the University of Central Florida, Joe and Justin were heading back to Texas, Ben was on his way back to Oregon, and Pete and Monica were going to vacation in City of Rocks, Idaho. One thing was for certain, though; this wouldn't be our last trip together. There was much left to do. We had pictures and trip reports to write up for our website and to send to W.L. Gore and Associates, money to raise, and training to do before sitting down and starting to plan out our next adventure. To where? We still don't know, but we will soon enough.

As the plane lifted off from the runway the next morning, I sat back and thought about Gannett Peak. Was our trip a success? Some people might say, "No, you didn't reach the summit." Others might say, "Yes." I might not have reached the summit personally, but I had grown as a climber and outdoorsman. I had become closer with already very close friends; I had suffered with these guys, and I knew that they would have my back 100 percent in any situation just as I knew I would have theirs in any situation. But at the same time, I turned in my seat and imagined the great spires of the Tetons disappearing below and behind us. "Don't worry, Gannett, I'll be back, and I will climb and summit you. I guarantee it."

Chapter 16

Love is Blind

"Love is blind, so you have to feel your way." —Brazilian Proverb

"Love may be blind, but it can sure find its way around in the dark. —unknown

"Love is the poetry of the senses." —Balzac

"So, Kyle and Andrew, how do you guys know if a girl's hot or not?" Brad asked. It was around 1 a.m., and we were all in our room during the retreat in Estes Park in March 2006. I was on a top bunk right above Andrew. Justin had claimed the queen-sized bed in the middle of the room. Ryan and Brad had the bunk on the opposite side of the room from Andrew and me.

Brad's question is one that many sighted people undoubtedly ask. Many think that since we can't see, surface beauty doesn't matter. Well, sorry to break the illusion, but blind guys are pigs too.

I don't know when exactly I started noticing girls. Probably not long after I watched my first James Bond 007 movie. I watched plenty of TV during my first six years and met countless girls and women, but I don't know if I knew what beautiful or ugly was. Emotions are complex, and I don't pretend to know much about it except that it's awkward talking about it when you're young. (Shoot, it's awkward talking about it as an adult.) Fortunately, one of my best childhood friends turned out to be quite knowledgeable and smooth when it came to the opposite sex.

Fishing Tales

I met John Norville when I was three or four years old. We met at church but didn't become friends until after my left eye was removed. John's dad was my family's realtor. Mom and Mrs. Norville were both very involved in church. One day, Dad and Mr. Norville decided to take their sons on a little fishing trip. It was just a little day trip fishing off a dock, but it was a chance for Mr. Norville and Dad to spend time with their sons and the sons to get to know each other.

John was a year older than I was, and Charlie, John's brother, was about five years older. I was shy and didn't know too much about fishing. But John did and showed me how to bait and cast a line. Before long, the day became more about talking, laughing, and throwing a football around than fishing. That night John asked me to spend the night at his house. My first sleepover.

That first sleepover would be one of many. We'd jump off the end of a twin bed in John's room and slam dunk a little orange ball through a basketball hoop that hung on the back of the door. And through playing together and sleepovers, John and I developed a friendship that has lasted a lifetime.

John visited me in the hospital the day after they removed my right eye. I'm sure he was scared and nervous. I sure was. How would we play now that I couldn't see? What would we do? Somehow, we figured it out.

It wasn't long, and we were playing just as fierce and joyously as we'd played when I had one eye. John took no mercy on me in whatever game or activity we were doing. Whether it was basketball, football, soccer, fishing, bike riding, or playing video games, we found a way to have fun without compensating too much for my blindness. And I loved every minute of it.

It was probably around fourth or fifth grade that John developed a talent for smooth-talking with the ladies. Quite often, he'd describe what he thought were the prettiest girls to me, whether that was at church, school, the mall, or just someone on the street. When I was in fifth, and John in sixth grade, John talked a lot about the cute girls at school. He promised that he'd let me know who the "hot girls" on the gifted track were, and he'd make sure I was "set up" with them. (Ah, John Norville. What a funny guy.)

Secret Handshakes

In fifth grade, I guess you could've called me the Big Man on Campus. Everyone knew me. I was student council president, one of the best drummers in the school band, was a rock climber, and had been on the Oprah Winfrey Show. I received several candy grams and cards from girls all over the school, but I didn't have the mad smooth-talking skills John did.

In middle school, John and I developed a secret handshake for John to let me know what girls were hot or not. We might be hanging out waiting for the bus, one of us talking to one or more girls. John would casually grab my hand, and depending on the grip; I'd know if the girl we were talking with was hot or not. We took the grips from Erik Weihenmayer's book—no need to reinvent the wheel.

When John grabbed my hand in a traditional handshake, that meant a girl was average-to-okay. If he grabbed my hand with his four fingers curled or hooked, that meant the girl was ugly. And if he grabbed my hand, interlocking our thumbs and wrapping his four fingers around the top of my hand, then she was hot!

John was my wingman but wasn't always around, so I taught the handshake to other buddies. If we were alone and there weren't any girls around, my friends would just tell me which girls were hot, what they looked like, and such. Whatever system we used, it worked nicely.

In seventh grade, there were many boys with a massive crush on our Language Arts teacher. She was younger, probably mid-20s, and according to all my buds, she was "HOT!" She had a smooth and sweet voice but could raise it and be strict if needed. That was around the time when it dawned on me that I didn't just need to rely on my friends to let me know if a girl was good-looking. I had my other senses, which I used in day-to-day life. Why not use them in terms of figuring out for myself whether girls were good-looking? I started listening.

Inner Voice

You can tell a lot from a voice. I tended to like a more soft-spoken person. If they passed the voice test, it was on to the hand, wrist, and/or elbow test.

A simple shake of the hand, touch on the wrist, or holding onto the elbow could tell me even more. Short, fat stubby fingers generally meant a short, fat stubby body. (Not my type.) I was more interested in the fit, athletic, and graceful — generally characterized by slender, but not skinny, fingers, wrists, and elbows.

But while I was developing these mad perceptual skills, I still lacked in the confidence department. Put me up on a rock wall, up on stage for a speech, or in front of a camera for a TV interview, and I had no trouble. But put me one-on-one or in a small group with a few girls, and I became almost mute.

I gained confidence in high school. Particularly in my senior year. During my sophomore and junior years, John, dad, and several other friends had been doing their best by giving me tips, hints. John and I went to several parties, and John would discreetly place me in the middle of a group of girls and casually throw out that I'd climbed a few mountains and was a wrestler.

With my senior year of high school, I was more confident and sure of myself. One big reason was my newest side-kick — Tyrone. Finally, I didn't have to use climbing or wrestling as a conversation starter. Walking in the halls at school, it was almost comical hearing girls "OOO"-ing and "Aww"-ing at the sight of Tyrone. It also didn't hurt that I was now the wrestling team captain and had worked hard on my physique. Maybe a few of the ooos and awwwws were for me. (Hey, I can dream, right?) With my new four-legged wingman, I was ready to break into the dating scene.

Dating Scene

In terms of actual romantic relationships, I didn't have many. During sophomore year, I became friends with Sarah. She was a pretty, soft-spoken, smart, and athletic girl. We had several classes together over sophomore and junior year, and I desperately wanted to ask her out. But she had a boyfriend, so I bided my time until she was single again.

We started hanging out more at school. But try as I might, I couldn't talk Sarah into going on a date. She did agree to go to prom with me. And on prom night, I gave it one more go asking if she'd just give me a chance and go out with me. She said she'd just prefer to be friends.

Getting turned down definitely hurt, but I learned from my unsuccessful stab at dating. I learned what signs to read and what not to read. I got better at developing relationships in general. And college was just around the corner. And as John told me, "There were plenty of fish in the sea." And I knew that the right girl was still out there for me.

Nice Voice

It was the start of my second year at UCF. I had a class on Thursday nights from 6 to 9 p.m., Interpersonal Communication. I had wrestling practice from 4 to 6 p.m., but because I had class, coach let me out at 5 p.m. I showered and made it to class just a couple of minutes early to grab a front-row seat.

What I didn't know at the time was that a pretty brunette sat down right behind me who had seen me waiting outside the classroom door and had an urge to get to know me. But she was a little shy. She took the seat behind me in hopes that she'd get a chance to talk with me later.

When our instructor, Dr. Ann Miller, called the roll, I heard a soft, sweet voice, right behind me, say, "Here." The voice belonged to Kailee, and I immediately liked the sound of her voice. I wondered if there would be an opportunity to talk to her at any point. I just wanted to hear that voice again.

Later, Dr. Miller separated us into groups. We counted off by fours. All ones were in a group, the twos in a group, and so on. When I met with my group, we couldn't quite get our schedules to mesh right. Dr.

Miller said she'd put me with another group. Kailee wasn't far from me when Dr. Miller said this and immediately said, "He can be in our group!" But Dr. Miller must not have heard her because I got put with another group.

It was the end of class, and whenever we finished up hashing out our schedules for future meetings with our groups, we could leave. Kailee had finished with her group and stepped outside to wait for me. We hadn't even introduced ourselves to each other yet, and she was waiting for me to come out of class just so she could get to know me. She waited there for about five minutes, and I didn't come out. I was still talking with my group about one thing or another. Another five minutes went by, and Kailee was feeling awkward. She was thinking, "What am I doing? Why am I waiting for a guy I don't even know?"

Finally, after about twelve, Kailee's wait was over. Tyrone and I came out and began speeding down the hall toward the doors to the outside. I had no idea that Kailee had been waiting for me. I didn't even know she was there until she came running up from behind me and asked, trying to disguise that she'd had to run to catch up with me, "What did you think of class?" It was the girl with the sweet voice.

I slowed my pace, and we began to talk. It was easy to talk with Kailee. She had the sweetest voice and most infectious smile and laugh I'd ever come across. We talked about anything and everything that came into our heads. We talked about class, what we were studying, our families. She genuinely seemed interested in me. Other girls that I'd talked to throughout my first year at UCF always started by asking me about Tyrone. When I met Tyrone, Sue, the trainer from The Seeing Eye, told me Tyrone would be a chick magnet. In my early introduction to getting to know girls, I took advantage of Tyrone being my wingman. After several years, though, I began to wonder if it was my Golden Retriever they were attracted to or me. Chalk that up to lacking in the confidence department, too.

But Kailee was different. I don't even think we talked about Tyrone that first night. I noticed it. And I liked it. Very much.

Before I knew it, we were standing at the crosswalk that would lead me back to my dorm. I regretfully told Kailee that my dorm was just a short walk away, and she said that she needed to get back to her car.

Before she left, I quickly said, "Look, I'm terrible with names, and I'm afraid I didn't catch yours when we started talking."

"No problem. It's Kailee," she said. I reached out my hand and clasped hers in mine. She had a small hand with a soft and gentle grip. And I knew that she was beautiful. She'd passed the voice and hand test, and two weeks later, Kailee passed the elbow test with flying colors.

Unfortunately, that night, Kailee had to walk back across campus to the building where we'd had class to get her car. But fortunately, one of the security people who drives around on a golf cart at UCF gave Kailee a lift back to her car so that she didn't have to walk. Once she got back to her apartment, Kailee called her mom and went on and on about this amazing guy she'd met in class. And her mom said, "You're going to marry that guy."

Brown-Eyed Girl

The following week, I was running a little late for class, skidding into class just before Dr. Miller closed the door. I wasn't sure if Kailee had taken the seat right behind me again or not. We didn't talk all class, but I was very careful to make sure that I walked much slower out the door when class was over. And to my delight, Kailee fell into step beside me. Our conversation flowed as easily as it had the previous week. And this week, Kailee had parked her car on the same side of campus as my dorm. When we made it to the crosswalk, I asked her to add me as a friend on Facebook. I'd searched for her several times, but there were several Kailee, and since I couldn't see the pictures, I couldn't determine which Kailee was the right one. She promised she'd add me, and we parted. For the next 30 minutes, I kept checking my computer, anxious to receive her friend request. Finally, it came. And we began sending Facebook messages back and forth.

I'd been learning what I could about Kailee through our conversations. I knew that she was majoring in Interdisciplinary Studies. Her parents were divorced. Her mom and little sister lived in North Carolina, and her dad was a firefighter in Palm Bay. Kailee had grown up in Palm Bay and loved the beach. In high school, she'd swam, run track and cross country, and lettered in all of them. When she got to UCF, she tried out for and made the women's rowing team. Through our Facebook messages, I learned that Kailee was a fan of country music, although one of her favorite songs was "Brown Eyed Girl" by Van Morrison. "There just aren't enough songs about us brown-eyed girls," she wrote to me. (So, she had brown eyes.)

The weekend we connected on Facebook, Kailee invited me to come with her and her dad to the first UCF home football game of the season. But unfortunately, I'd already planned on going home that weekend. I regretfully said I couldn't go, but I hoped we could hang out soon.

When we came out of class for the third week in a row, Kailee mentioned that she was a little hungry. I jumped at the chance to spend even more time with her. And since I hadn't eaten after wrestling practice, I was ravenous. I asked if she wanted to go to Subway.

Now, I'll be honest. I knew how to get to Subway. But I pulled the smooth blind guy move. I said to her, "I am not exactly sure where Subway is. Would it be all right if I held your elbow so you can guide me?"

Smooth, huh?

Well, of course, she said that was okay with her. I reached my hand out, and I wrapped my fingers around her elbow and confirmed what I already knew—she was the sexy athletic type.

Nice.

We sat, ate, and talked for over an hour before getting up and walking to my dorm. This time Kailee walked all the way to the front door of my dorm. Before she left, I pulled out my phone and asked if she could plug her name and number into it so I could call her some time. After typing in her information and giving me back the phone, she threw her arms around my neck, giving me a huge hug. I put my arms around her and knew I couldn't wait to ask her out. I called her the next day and asked her to come and hang out with me at my dorm on Sunday. She did.

She came over in the early afternoon. I had the Jacksonville Jaguars football game streaming through my computer but wasn't paying attention to it. Kailee and I just sat on my bed, talking, laughing, and enjoying being together. Then on an impulse, I leaned forward and kissed her.

We held the kiss for several seconds, and then, feeling a little silly and embarrassed, I pulled back and said, "You don't have a boyfriend, right?"

She laughed and said, "No."

"Well, then would you like to go out with me, and I can be your boyfriend?" For an answer, she leaned forward and kissed me. "I'll take that as a yes."

One Knee

From that day on, Kailee and I hardly spent a day apart. Unless one of us needed to be alone to study, was in class, or I was at wrestling practice, we were together. Just being together made us happy. A month after we started dating, Kailee and I drove up to Amelia Island to introduce Kailee to my family — and John Norville, of course. After John met Kailee, he pulled me aside — out of her earshot — and said, "Kyle, you're a lucky man. She's gorgeous!"

Kailee got along great with my parents and three sisters. Even my dad's goofy jokes didn't scare her off. A week later, I met Kailee's dad. We immediately hit it off when he told me that he'd just gotten back from a two-week canoe trip down the Suwanee River.

Kailee and I just grew closer over the next year. Sure, we had our moments where we didn't agree on one thing or another, and I found out that Kailee could be very stubborn and feisty. But she was just as beautiful feisty as she was when she was laughing. I knew that I wanted to spend the rest of my life listening to her talk, holding her in my arms, and kissing her. I had a long talk with my parents and told them that I wanted to ask Kailee to marry me. They approved and couldn't wait for Kailee to join our family. I pride myself on being a Southern gentleman; before I popped the question, I had to ask Randy, Kailee's dad, for his permission.

I have a second cousin who's a director for ESPNU, and he'd invited me to the 2012 College Football Red Carpet and Awards show. Since Randy and I were huge football fans, I asked Randy to come with me. We spent the day meeting some of the biggest names in college football, getting pictures and autographs. And as we drove home in Randy's truck, I asked him for Kailee's hand. He shook my hand and said that I had his permission and blessing, and it would be an honor to have me as a son-in-law. Now I just needed to plan how to ask Kailee to marry me.

The week before Christmas, I went up to Jacksonville to spend some time with my family, and Kailee flew up to North Carolina to visit her mom and sister. While in Jacksonville, mom, dad, and I went to the jeweler that my dad uses whenever he buys mom or my sisters a Christmas or birthday present. They described the different engagement rings to me, and the person helping us let me touch them as well. I finally found the perfect ring for Kailee and bought it.

Now it was just a matter of hiding the ring from Kailee until January 1, 2013, when I planned on asking her. Kailee and I both got back to Orlando a couple of days before Christmas. We spent Christmas together. I hid the ring as best I could and prayed that Kailee wouldn't accidentally come across it.

Randy's mother, Kailee's grandmother, whom everyone calls Mana, owned a rental house on the Santa Fe River not far outside Gainesville. Kailee and I'd visited Mana several times throughout the year and a half we'd been dating, and we both loved it, the way of life, the peace and quiet, and the family atmosphere. Mana had mentioned several times that I should invite my family to come and stay at the "Springhouse" (her rental house) so that our families could get to know one another better. Mana booked the Springhouse for my parents and sisters on January first and second. Kailee and I drove up the day before and visited with Mana. The next day, Randy and his girlfriend and my parents, and three sisters arrived. We had a fun time talking, joking and just having fun. I'd had the ring in my pocket for the entire day, looking for an opportunity to propose to Kailee.

I kept asking if she wanted to get away and go for a little walk—just the two of us—but whenever it seemed she'd be ready, something would grab her attention, and we'd be talking with someone else. Finally, I told Kailee, "Look, we need to take a walk. Just you and me." She wasn't quite sure what was going on. She later told me that she thought I would tell her something bad like I'd been diagnosed with some new form of cancer or that I was moving away or something.

I took her hand, and we walked a little ways. I asked her to find a pretty spot on the riverbank. We found the spot and sat down. I put my arm around her, pulling her close, and told her how much I loved her and how I'd always love her. I told her how we had something special and that I wanted to be with her. Then I told her that I had something to give her, and I asked her to stand up. Down on one knee, I pulled the ring box out of my pocket, opened it up, and asked, "Kailee, will you marry me?"

I'd barely gotten the words out when Kailee said, "Yes!" I slipped the ring on her finger and held her close as she cried tears of happiness.

Neither of us knew what the future held for us. But we knew that we wanted to be together when we found out. Kailee's was my everything. She brightened up each and every day. I would climb and stand on the summits of all the mountains in the world, and the feeling of love, happiness, and joy wouldn't compare to a day with Kailee.

It didn't take a secret handshake or inside information from my buddies or a four-legged chick magnet to tell me when I found the woman meant for me. All I had to do was listen and feel. That's all I needed. Because love, truly, is blind.

Chapter 17

Welcome TO THE Real World

"70 percent of people who are blind or visually impaired are either not employed or severely under-employed."

"More than 56 percent of people who are blind or visually impaired have post-secondary education degrees."

I knew the statistics, but I didn't think they'd apply to me. I was Kyle Coon, the blind guy who overcame the obstacles in my way by sheer determination. I learned the hard way that the real world could be fun and hurt way more than I could have imagined.

"It's not the grades you make; it's the hands you shake," my childhood friend John Norville would often tell me as we drove around Jacksonville in his car. I remember laughing at this statement. How can you expect to get a good job if you don't have good grades? That's all I knew. Hard work was getting As and Bs; if I did that, getting a job part of life would be easy.

I graduated from the University of Central Florida with a bachelor's degree in Interpersonal/Organizational Communication. In simpler terms, that meant I could write a pretty good research paper and knew about a few communication theories. I'd chosen communication because I felt it would help my writing ability and because it was so broad that it wouldn't limit me to a career path. After graduating, I discovered that my degree was so broad that I couldn't pinpoint what I wanted to do.

During my last semester at UCF, a professor, Joan McCain, organized a student team for an independent study that branded me as a motivational speaker. At the same time, Joan was working with me on writing what would become this book. I learned a ton working with Joan and the other students on the independent study, and I still have much of the material they developed to help brand me as a speaker. But unfortunately, I didn't make much use of it for a while. I picked up a few minor speaking engagements, but not enough to help support me or the future family I hoped to have with Kailee.

At the time, I was also interested in taking Team Sight Unseen further, maybe making it into a nonprofit similar to Global Explorers. To help me prepare for this, I enrolled in a graduate certificate program for nonprofit management. Halfway through my first class on grant writing, I learned that nonprofit management wasn't for me, and I withdrew from the program. Or maybe I was just tired of school. After going through the grind of Paxon for four years and then getting my bachelor's in three years, I felt like I'd been in school forever, and I wanted to make money.

Job Hunting

At the time, I worked as a group exercise instructor at the UCF Recreation and Wellness Center and enjoyed what I did. So, I started applying to gyms and fitness clubs all over Orlando, trying to get full-time or a couple of part-time positions. No response. I wrote and rewrote my resume and cover letters. I tried leveraging my blindness as an asset. When that didn't work, I stopped saying I was blind altogether.

Eventually, I abandoned pursuing a career in the health and fitness industry and started applying for jobs in the marketing and communication fields. I started applying for every job I could find in the Orlando area. I sent out hundreds of resumes and wrote dozens of cover letters, only receiving the occasional call or interview. Sometimes the interviews went well, but I'd not hear back about a second interview, starting the search all over again.

The process continued for six or more months after I graduated, and I started to get a little discouraged. I read any book that I thought could give me an edge: self-help, resume, business, entrepreneurship, psychology, finance, and such. Randy, Kailee's dad, bought me a brand-new suit for Christmas and insisted that it would give me more confidence.

For a while, it did. I did feel more confident strolling into an interview with a nice suit on with a badass resume in hand and a good-looking guide dog leading me. But for some reason, my confidence wasn't convincing potential employers.

First Impressions

I remember a series of interviews in the early part of 2014 in particular. I'd applied for a marketing/public relations position through an online job site and was contacted very quickly for an interview. I arrived at the interview early with my resume in hand and Tyrone strutting alongside me as he's one to do. But as I stepped up to the receptionist to check-in, she appeared to be in a bad mood or something. After she helped me sign in, I went and sat down to wait my turn for the interview. I interviewed with a couple of managers and thought the interview went well. They said they'd contact me regarding a second interview. I left feeling hopeful.

As I stood outside waiting for my ride, another candidate who'd been sitting next to me in the lobby came out and asked me how my interview went and if I'd gotten a second interview. I said that I thought the interview had gone well, and they said they'd contact me regarding a second interview. She appeared a bit surprised as she said, "Oh, well, they offered me a second interview right away." And as she walked away, I wondered if I was just bad at interviewing or if it was something else. I pushed it from my mind.

I never was called back for a second interview but applied for another job with a company that shared the same office space. This company immediately called me for an interview. As I walked into the reception area, the receptionist asked, "What are you doing here?" When I explained that I had a job interview, she excused herself and asked me to have a seat. I did, and five minutes later, she came out and said that the hiring manager had just been called into an emergency meeting and would call me to reschedule my interview. I was stunned, especially since I'd just gotten off the phone with the hiring manager 30 minutes earlier confirming my interview. I left beyond confused.

I returned to that building two or three more times to interview with different companies that shared the same office space receiving the same frosty reception by the receptionist. Only once did I interview, and I received no second interview.

Almost Broken

It was now approaching a year since I'd graduated from college, and I was starting to panic as I applied all over the country, desperately trying to find something. My friend and mentor, Erik Weihenmayer, wrote a blog post about my job-seeking struggles. I obtained a teaching certificate to teach Earth and Space Science, but there were no Earth and Space Science teaching positions open anywhere I looked. I was starting to spiral downward fast. My stress level went up and all this combined to put a great strain on my personal relationships with my family and with Kailee.

When I get stressed, I tend to both eat and sleep a lot. Kailee would come home from work to find me passed out on the couch with my laptop either open on my lap or lying on the floor next to me. She tried to be understanding, but gradually her patience wore thin. She started dropping hints that I should bite the bullet and go back to get my master's degree and become a Community College or University professor. Then my parents started dropping hints that I should think about moving back to Jacksonville to find a job there.

I was desperate to find a job in Orlando to be with Kailee and start making money. So, I went and applied for the one job I felt sure I'd get. I went to the supermarket and applied to be a bag boy. I went through two interviews without being hired. After that, I felt nearly hopeless. If I wasn't good enough to be a bag boy, then what was the use of trying to go back to school to get a Master's degree or do anything at all?

I was now so deep in credit card debt and desperate for money that I applied for Social Security Benefits. As someone who is totally blind,

I could apply and receive benefits as long as I made less than $1,820 per month. After completing and submitting the paperwork, I received word that they determined my liquid assets were enough to live on, so they denied my application. The Roth IRA and investment accounts that my dad had set up for me several years earlier were the reasons for this determination. Social Security said that I could liquidate those, and I wouldn't need their money. But if I liquefied, then I'd really have nothing. I hated the idea of living off the government and didn't fight the SSA's decision to deny me benefits. I was on the verge of a total meltdown and ready to pull the trigger to move back to Jacksonville and try my luck at finding a job in my hometown.

But when we've reached our lowest point is when the opportunities are greatest.

Small Encounters

In April 2014, I attended a luncheon honoring people featured on Central Florida News 13's "Every Day Hero" segment. I'd been featured not long after graduating from UCF when I still had big plans for Sight Unseen and myself. Now, I was just a shell of that confident college grad. I certainly didn't feel like an "Everyday Hero." I was jobless, practically penniless, and was pretty much out of hope for my future in central Florida. Little did I know how pivotal that luncheon would be for me.

Kailee and Randy had to work the day of the luncheon, so my parents drove down from Jacksonville to attend with me. We enjoyed our lunch and enjoyed talking with our tablemates, but I really just wanted to get home, take my suit off, and hopelessly keep looking for jobs. A few tables away, a man named Kyle Johnson spotted me with Tyrone under my chair, and then he saw my name in the program.

While I stood outside the luncheon room waiting for my parents to return from the restroom, Kyle Johnson walked up to me and introduced himself. He was the Director of Sustainability and Communication for Lighthouse Central Florida—a nonprofit agency in Orlando that provides vision-specific rehabilitation services for the blind and visually impaired. I knew of Lighthouse, having received orientation and mobility training from them, but apart from that didn't know much about them. Kyle asked if we could exchange contact information and maybe have a cup of coffee as he wanted to talk to me about possibly speaking at a Lighthouse fundraiser later that year. We exchanged contact info and agreed to keep in touch.

Some weeks went by before we arranged to have that cup of coffee. We met at a Starbucks near where I was living with Kailee and Randy. I told Kyle my story, and he asked if I'd be interested in speaking at Lighthouse's annual fundraiser. I said it would be an honor. Then as we started wrapping up our meeting, he asked what I did for a living. I told him, "Nothing. I can't find a job."

"Send me your resume, and I'll see if I can spread it around and keep an ear to the ground for you," he said.

As soon as I got home, I sent off my resume to Kyle Johnson. At the time, I didn't know that he had no intention of spreading my resume around. He later told me that he just printed off my resume, walked it down to the CFO's office, and said, "We need to hire this guy." Two weeks later, I was employed.

Lighthouse Works

In 2011, Lighthouse Central Florida formed a subsidiary corporation called Lighthouse Works. The goal of Lighthouse Works was two-fold. First, they wanted to provide meaningful employment to people who are blind or visually impaired. Second, the revenue generated by Lighthouse Works would then be funneled back into Lighthouse Central Florida so it could be a self-sustaining nonprofit and therefore rely less on private donations and government grants. This structure is known as a social enterprise nonprofit. It's a nonprofit that makes a profit to assist the parent nonprofit.

Lighthouse Works started as a call center and employed a few blind or visually impaired people. They contracted with companies to do telemarketing and quality assurance. Then they developed a supply chain and fulfillment division and contracted with the Defense

Logistics Agency to source and fulfill items in the "Combat Life Saver Kit," which contains emergency medical supplies that one-in-five to one-in-eight soldiers carry. In June 2014, they were still a young operation but were on a positive trajectory for growth.

I walked into a small lobby in downtown Orlando and introduced myself to the front desk person. He asked me to have a seat, and he contacted Travis Morris—the Call Center Manager with whom I'd be interviewing. Travis then came out and led me back to the room where I'd interview. Then he and Dee Amundson—Lighthouse's Director of Finance and HR—proceeded to go through a list of interview questions. We talked about my work experience, goals and ambitions, technical experience, computer and telephone experience.

I held nothing back. I didn't really want to be a call center agent, but I needed this opportunity. I let them know that I had ambition, and I wanted to move up in the world and pull my own weight.

Travis later joked that it wasn't my drive or abilities that got me the job, but the fact that in 2003 I'd appeared on the Oprah Winfrey Show as a surprise guest to Erik Weihenmayer. I later learned that Travis is a huge Oprah fan.

Late that night, I received a call from Travis asking if I could start the following Monday. Without hesitation, I said, "Yes!" I had my first full-time job.

Moving Up

My first few weeks on the job focused on learning about the organization, learning how to use the phones, and learning about what I'd be doing. I quickly developed a talent for quality assurance. My supervisor—a totally blind woman named Sharon—worked with me on customer service skills and what to listen for, and how to write coaching notes providing constructive feedback.

The call center—named the 4Sight360 Call Center—also had a contract that dealt with developing mystery shopping scenarios for booking moderate to large events or conventions. I became very good at creating the mystery shopping scenarios that we call center agents would use to "shop" the hotel. We'd record the calls, and then I'd listen to the call in full, score, and provide constructive feedback to the hotel sales rep who was supposed to be booking the event.

The 4Sight360 Call Center was separated into two centers: inbound and outbound. I worked primarily in the outbound call center. The inbound call center was composed primarily of agents with severe visual impairments. They worked on a campaign where they took inbound calls for a local medical network scheduling doctor appointments. Lighthouse's in-house software developer—Mike Fox—was in the process of making the softphone (an internet-based telephone system) and scheduling software compatible with JAWS so that a totally blind person could take and schedule medical appointments as well. Eventually, he succeeded in writing a completely new program that allowed JAWS to interact with multiple software and potentially make the proficient JAWS user more efficient than a sighted or partially sighted agent.

Lighthouse decided to initially test this ground-breaking software with a few select totally blind agents who'd been with Lighthouse for a while. They also needed Spanish speakers. The current front desk manager—a man named Eddie Torres—was totally blind and bilingual in English and Spanish, so they pulled him from his front desk duty to test JAWS with the softphone and scheduling software. Travis and Sharon decided to move me from the call center to the front desk.

The switch was a good move for me. I still had to maintain all the quality assurance evaluations and other projects I was managing in addition to front desk duties. Having proven myself adept at quality assurance (QA), they then tasked me with managing the QA Evaluations for our Lighthouse inbound call center team. This new task was a full-time endeavor in and of itself. I was already performing 50 QA evaluations a month for one contract we had with a water and sewer company. Now I was asked to take on 100 to 120 more QA evaluations in addition to that.

I took it in stride and became very good at efficiently knocking out evaluations and getting them to Travis by the end of each month. But now, I was also performing front desk duties—checking people in, taking inbound phone calls from people asking about the services of Lighthouse Central Florida, greeting important visitors who were there to meet with upper management, and much more. I stayed busy.

Over the next year and a half, I continued working diligently. I took on even more responsibilities and liked to think that I helped Lighthouse Central Florida and Lighthouse Works grow. I became Lighthouse's first Advocacy Coordinator. As such, I communicated with officials at the city, county, state, and federal levels of government. I assisted in forming Lighthouse's first Public Policy Committee, whose goal is to stay abreast of political and social issues and how those issues may affect Lighthouse's mission. I also got many opportunities to speak at civic organizations such as Rotary Clubs.

I made enormous strides in my professional life, eventually leaving Lighthouse to work as a civilian for the Department of the Navy. It was a new challenge and a significant raise in pay. But while I climbed the ladder of success in my professional life, my personal life left much to be desired.

Cancer, Round 2

I started working for Lighthouse in June 2014. By then, Kailee and I'd been engaged for a year and a half. She was excited that I finally had a job, and we briefly discussed starting to plan a wedding once I settled into my new job. After a couple of months on the job, I went to the doctor to check a bump on my upper right eyelid that had been bothering me for a while.

My doctor sent me to a dermatologist who biopsied the bump. A week later, he informed me that I had a rare form of skin cancer called a sebaceous gland carcinoma. If left untreated, the consequences were not pleasant. However, the dermatologist was confident that I'd pull through. Even though I knew he was probably right, my heart still seemed to stop when I heard the word "cancer," and I immediately thought, "Not again!"

After consulting with my former ophthalmologist from Jacksonville and the Shields-in Philadelphia-we determined that the carcinoma was a secondary cancer that resulted from the extensive external beam radiation treatment I'd undergone as a kid. My ophthalmologist, Dr. Hered, recommended a Jacksonville surgeon he'd worked with previously—Dr. Costick. After a quick visit and assessment with Dr. Costick, I was scheduled for surgery to remove my upper right eyelid.

In October 2014, Kailee drove me to Jacksonville, where I underwent surgery and then spent a couple of days recuperating before returning to Orlando and work. Before surgery, Kailee and I were feeling some strain in our relationship, despite our marriage talks. She appeared to be a little resentful and frustrated that it had taken me so long to find work after graduating. She was already a successful seventh-grade teacher and supporting our little family—her, me, and Tyrone. Once I got my job at Lighthouse, I picked up a few bills and did my best, but only making $10 an hour before taxes meant I wasn't exactly raking in the dough.

My second cancer diagnosis seemed to push those lingering frustrations away as Kailee threw herself into helping me recover. I hoped we could grow closer again as we had been before I graduated from college.

What happened next was a conflagration of rash decisions and unintended consequences that, when I look back, I probably could've prevented if I'd kept my head and thought rationally.

Coming Apart

Once I'd sufficiently recovered from surgery, Kailee and I decided that we were sick and tired of waiting to get married. No, I didn't have the most financially secure job in the world, but we'd waited long enough, and we were just ready to be married. We decided to do something small with our parents and a notary. We set a date for December 13, 2014.

A marriage is between two people on a piece of paper. But planning a wedding involves more than two people. The devil, as they say, is in the details. And details proved to be the undoing for Kailee and me.

We had a date. It changed.

Then the month changed six months farther down the road.

Then the date changed again to January 1 to commemorate the day we got engaged. In the wave of sentimentality and the excitement, people were told, Facebook events created, and momentum started before we realized my parents could not attend on that date due to their long-planned move to Colorado and the requirements of their new housing arrangements.

Next came questions about changing the date. Feelings were hurt. Tears flowed. Tempers flared. Words exchanged. It was heated.

I was confused. I didn't know what was going on. For me, it was a ping pong match of emotions bouncing around between a family who had always been there for me and a woman I loved whom I wanted with me for the rest of my life. I shut down.

Finally, I called off the wedding until we could sort out the mess. Kailee was angry. My family was angry. And I didn't know what to do.

Kailee and I had a very frosty Christmas and New Year's. It was like there was a void that had opened between us. I made some half-hearted attempts to bridge the gap and understand what had happened. I threw myself into work and exercising, trying to drown my self-doubt and heartache with outside distractions.

It didn't work.

Soon Kailee started staying later and later at work and going out with friends more and more. We stopped going on dates, and eventually, we stopped talking. To the outside world, though, we appeared to be trying to work things out. In reality, we weren't trying as hard as we probably could have.

For eight months, we struggled through what we'd become until one night Kailee simply said, "We can't keep doing this." I agreed.

Just like that, it was over.

All my plans, hopes, and dreams seemed to disappear. I was empty with a hollowness where my heart used to be.

I'd started racing triathlons earlier that year with a friend, Mike, whom I'd met through a website that connected blind athletes with people who wanted to be guides. Mike and I hit it off and were soon running half marathons, marathons, and triathlons together. Strangely enough, Mike was also going through a rough breakup, and he offered me a spot in his house while we both tried to sort out our messed-up love lives. For several months after breaking up with Kailee, I struggled. I put on a brave face to the world, saying that I was just relieved to not be in limbo anymore. But I was hurting.

It took me a long time to sort out my feelings. The end of my engagement wasn't any one person or group's fault. It was just one more viciously hard, an unexpected obstacle in my life.

And while I hurt from it, it ultimately made me a stronger person. I wish nothing but the best for Kailee, and I won't ever say a bad thing against her. We're both good people and undoubtedly will find our matches. We just turned out to not be a perfect match for each other. That is the story of my entrance into the "real world." Much like everything else in my life, it was hardcore. It was challenging. Yet, I came out the other side in one piece and stronger for it.

On to the next summit.

Epilogue: Time to Tri

"Kyle, I think you can do an Ironman," Mike said one day as we ran along together.

"Dude, that's like swimming, biking, and running. I can barely run."

"Trust me, man. Just give it a tri."

My engagement officially ended in July 2015. One year earlier, I'd met Mike Melton, an ER doctor who was training for the Ironman World Championships in Kailua-Kona, Hawaii. Ironman—2.4-mile swim, 112-mile bike, 26.2-mile run. Who on Earth was crazy enough to do something that dumb?

In October 2014, I sat on the couch eagerly awaiting updates on my phone via the Ironman Tracker app as Mike battled big waves in Kailua Bay, vicious crosswinds on the Queen Ka'ahumanu Highway, and suffered oppressive heat in the Energy Lab. Of course, these names and places meant little to me at the time. All I knew was that a dude I'd been running with for three months was swimming 2.4 miles, biking 112 miles, and running a 26.2-mile marathon, and he had to do it in under 17 hours to be considered an official finisher. And 16 hours and 51 minutes after he started, Mike crossed the finish line on Alii Drive. Here's the thing, Mike's not a super athlete. Apart from some massive calves, you actually wouldn't think he's an endurance athlete. He's just a regular guy with an incredible bulldog mentality. In other words, my kind of guy.

When I graduated from UCF, I was ready to take on the world. I was the stereotypical millennial thinking I was hot shit, and I could just walk into any job and succeed. One denied application after another, one fruitless job interview after the other, and I started falling apart. I drank way more than necessary. I gained a significant amount of weight. And I lost my sense of identity.

I don't know what made me wake up one day and decide that I needed to make a change in my life. All I knew was that I had to do something that would give me a sense of purpose. I needed to put my money where my mouth was and actually live the message I'd been preaching my whole life.

I knew that my saving grace had always been some form of physical activity. I had little money, so getting to the closest rock climbing gym wasn't an option. I didn't have a stationary bike and didn't want to shell out the money to get one. I figured I'd do the one thing I'd always hated, but that was simple: running.

I knew I needed to find a running partner. I found a website that partnered blind athletes with sighted running guides. There were two people listed in the Orlando area as being interested/willing to guide blind runners. I emailed them both, and one of them responded.

In June 2014, I met Dr. Michael Melton. He'd never guided a blind runner before, and I had no idea what I was doing, but we both decided just to try this out. We started running together regularly. Then Mike signed me up for a 15K road race. Then a half marathon, a marathon, and finally, after months of peer pressure convinced me that triathlon was the way to go. And in April 2015, I crossed the finish line of my first Olympic distance triathlon—The St. Anthony's Triathlon in St. Petersburgh, Florida. It took me nearly three and a half hours to swim 1,500 meters, bike 40 kilometers, and run/walk 10 kilometers—all guided by Mike—but the sense of accomplishment I felt upon crossing the finish line and the excruciating pain I felt for days afterward told me that I was alive and I'd found a way to continue living my life without limits. Maybe that 2.4-mile swim, 112-mile bike, and 26.2-mile run weren't so dumb after all. Maybe Mike was right. Maybe I could be an Ironman. Maybe I just needed to Tri.

I've lived a full and adventurous life thus far. I like to think that I've lived my life without limits. And I'd like for all of you to strive to do the same.

Living a life without limits means something different to everyone. For me, it means pushing myself to get better every single day. I want to be a great athlete, friend, son, brother, writer, scholar, and much more. And in pursuing my best, I've encountered some adversity along the way. Blindness is something that certainly challenges me every day of my life. And while blindness was extremely difficult to handle at first, I have learned to accept it as a part of me.

Something Erik Weihenmayer taught me was to embrace the adversity we face. We often hear of people "overcoming" or "dealing with" adversity. I don't think these phrases quite capture the true essence of living with adversity.

Adversity, like life, is ongoing. It changes from day to day and presents us with numerous choices to make. My mom's favorite phrase is "Make good choices." She'd say this little phrase to us kids any time we'd leave the house—whether we were going to school, a friend's house, a party, or off to college. It was her way of reminding us that we would be presented with choices throughout our days and throughout our lives, and the choices we made would affect the path of our lives.

Did we always make the best of choices? No. I've made many bad choices over the years, and undoubtedly I'll probably make a few more. But when I make those bad choices, I do my best to analyze and learn from them.

Living a life without limits is about making the best choice available to you at a given moment. And it's learning from your mistakes. It's also not being afraid to take a chance or risk.

My parents took a chance in electing not to have my eyes removed less than a week after I was diagnosed with cancer. That decision gave me six years of decent sight and some great opportunities and family memories. Then, when I went blind, they decided not to baby me and forced me to be independent. It was hard for them to watch me struggle at times, but I learned to be a problem solver.

Success has come to me in many different forms. I was successful in academics and athletics—although not as successful as I wanted at the time. And I've been relatively successful thus far in my pursuit of outdoor adventure activities. When Brad Jaffke, Justin Grant, and I formed Team Sight Unseen, we agreed that "It's not the destination but the journey that makes the trip worthwhile." I've learned how to live my life to the fullest extent. And by no means am I done.

Erik Weihenmayer showed me the trailhead. My family, friends, and teachers have helped me along the way, but it's my choice to keep on climbing and to keep looking forward. Every time I crest a ridge on my life's journey, there always seems to be one a little higher. It's a longer, steeper, and more difficult journey to get there, but that's what makes the journey so remarkable.

What's next? Well, since 2015, triathlon has been my primary athletic focus. Since then, I've completed numerous triathlons ranging in distance and difficulty from sprint to Ironman. I didn't include those adventures in this book because my triathlon life could be a book in and of itself. In fact...

Maybe it will be.

One thing's for sure, though, I am just starting to live my life without limits. Cancer may have taken my sight. But the adversity of blindness gave me a new vision. And the mountains have let me live an exciting and fulfilling life thus far.

And I challenge you to do the same.

You don't need to go out and climb mountains. But don't pigeonhole yourself and make excuses. The time to step outside our comfort zones, face our fears, embrace adversity, and live a full and rewarding life is now!

As we close out this book, I'd like to summarize with you the lessons I've learned in the form of some of my favorite quotes. I look to these when I need a boost or reminder to keep forging ahead.

Until we meet again: Keep living your life without limits.

Quotes and Lessons:

"Every day's a holiday, every meal's a feast, and every paycheck's a fortune." —Steven Coon/Victor Sciullo

"There's no crime in not reaching your goal but only in failing to set one." —Ken Chertow

"Goals seem like false summits. You reach the top of one just to find another one a little higher."—Erik Weihenmayer

"Leadership equals vision plus action, the divisor is character." —Eric Alexander

"The real beauty of life happens on the side of a mountain; not the top." —Erik Weihenmayer

"You can wish in one hand and shit in the other. See which one fills up first." —Chris Morris

"If ifs, ands, and buts were candy and nuts, we'd all have a Merry fucking Christmas." —Chris Morris

"It's all about ambition and fear. Ambition is the overwhelming desire to get to the top, but fear will keep you alive." —Jeff Evans

"Bashed elbows and knees mean you're climbing hard." —Hans Florine

"Athletes compete with each other. Champions compete with themselves." —Ken Chertow

"The nature of mind is like water. If you do not disturb it, it will become clear." —Ancient Tibetan Saying

"I can walk into the door a hundred times, but until I turn the doorknob, it ain't gonna open." —Victor Sciullo

"If you think, laugh and cry you've had a full day." —Jim Valvano

"Don't go around saying the world owes you a living. The world owes you nothing. It was here first." —Mark Twain

"The future belongs to those who see possibilities before they become obvious." —John Sculley

"Quit your whining. It builds character." —Steven Coon

"It's our attitude that allows us to learn from mistakes and that in turn enables one to be great beyond imagination." —Steven Coon

"Make good choices." —Ann Marie Coon

To keep up with my latest adventures, please check out my website and give me a follow across all my social media channels:

Website: www.kylecoon.com
Facebook: www.facebook.com/kylecoonspeaks
Instagram: www.instagram.com/eyeronkyle
Twitter: www.twitter.com/kyle_coon